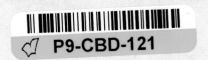

Also by Albert Goldbarth

COMINGS BACK

COMINGS BACK

a sequence of poems

by

Albert Goldbarth

Doubleday & Company, Inc.
Garden City, New York
1976

Library of Congress Cataloging in Publication Data

Goldbarth, Albert.
  COMINGS BACK.

  I. Title.
PS3557.0354C57   811'.5'4
ISBN: 0-385-11542-3
Library of Congress Catalog Card Number 76-2775

Acknowledgment is gratefully made to the editors of the following journals, not only for first publishing some of the poems in this volume, but for helping keep literature alive and available in often difficult times:

"Wire" and "Life Stories Of The Artists," in *The American Poetry Review*, Vol. 4, No. 1, 1975, Copyright © 1975 by The American Poetry Review; "John & The Lusitania," in *The American Poetry Review*, Vol. 4, No. 5, 1975, Copyright © by The American Poetry Review, 1975; "Europe Makes It Through the Plague," in *The Ark River Review*, Vol. 3, No. 2 & 3, Summer 1976, Copyright © by The Ark River Review, 1976; "Five Grumbles," in *The Beloit Poetry Journal*, Vol. 25, No. 2, Winter 1974–75, Copyright © 1974 by The Beloit Poetry Journal; "Narrative Continuity" and "For The Day," in *The Beloit Poetry Journal*, Vol. 24, No. 4, Summer 1974, Copyright © 1974 by The Beloit Poetry Journal; "Synecdoche: A Survey," in *The Black Warrior Review*, Vol. 2, No. 1, Fall 1975, Copyright © 1975 by The Black Warrior Review; "Clotting/Dear Ginnie:" in *Boundary* 2, Vol. 4, No. 1, Fall 1975, Copyright © 1975 by Boundary 2; "Song: Simple Truths" (originally published as "Some True Things After Talarico"), in *The Carolina Quarterly*, Vol. 26, No. 2,

CONTENTS

Grants from the National Endowment for the Arts
and the Illinois Arts Council
and a 1975 *Ark River Review* First Prize in Poetry
have aided in the completion of this manuscript.

for
those mentioned

Pooh, *promise* you won't forget about me, ever.

—Christopher Robin
in A. A. Milne's
The House at Pooh Corner

COMINGS BACK

Some Poems Around Some Lights

*So this scientist has a seat for this skeleton
and the lady what serves you was mad.
So do you know then what,
she took the bones and throwed them
out of the airplane window and that's
the joke.*

✳

And the drop
is endless. Not even Earth
stops it.
      If time is measured
by change, a prism is more
light-years than Alpha Centauri; a hand's-length
of Olduvai, longer
than a parachute knows. And every day,
child, here's a riddle, your grandmother sinks
deeper into the Earth
without moving.
          For Earth
leaps on top.
        And Earth
leaps on top.
         An apartment building
is archaeology, stratum
by stratum —so long
as there are ceilings, basements will go down to diamond;
mattresses stained
with our glandular dyes
will be Fossil Hotel. Another name
for dynasty
is *layers*. Now

✳

it's the Earth who's on top her
and moist at her thighs.

3

It's 1934, and the dishes are done. My father
steps out on the porch, the one
from the pictures, on Evergreen Avenue, and breathes
his neighborhood in: bronze clouds
of soup, a paint factory, the regiment tomatoes.
Then,
steps back, 6:00, and what's left
of the family undoes its spats and apron-snaps
and gathers round . . .
He sits down in front of *his* father's skull
now yellowed, and polished
to teak, and clicks on the faceless announcer
Radiocarbon,
streaming out, filling the air with the news.

At Juneway Beach, that huge soup
of stone and silver-green lake smelt, that
process, I thought
the Chicago Ten-Dollar Flotilla up:
a hundred balloons, with a hundred
keychain-flashlights clicked glowing inside, and
launched
for a gravity-bound constellation.
                                        /I wanted
a woman near me, columnar warmth
in my arms, to look in the tidepools and mean
the difference between our bones and whatever
calcium's in lakewater./
                        And we'd pump,
and knot, and watch them move out
on the wind and the turning planet.

Brick by brick walls darken and
the windows come out. Like the moon that was there
all along but it needed the gradual purpling
of air, the windows burn
back the night, a city block is so many heavy
packages of wattage. Here: it's the old
west side. It's a walking
blind, through black now, but
for the ancient myths that men have set
in lights: the Stew
in the Oven; the Slant of a Lamp
on a Book; the one Bare Scorch
in the Bedroom. It's
a neighborhood, and this for a man
in the gas and black glaze of a city street
is its guiding: the stories
the windows connect. It's
before transistors but every pane frames three
generations in miniature. It's
1934. If we had money, from the air
this would stun us.

4 A.M.; in the bedroom
above mine, bodies clang
together like tankers, and ride
the loud wash. But
what the lecture on geomorphology wants
for the overhead-projector is *my* body, where
the thigh is a long raw
siamese unjoining, and a hand
on the chalk-white promontory
of wrist-bone waves continually
good-bye. This is the theory
of continental drift, proved by paleomagnetism,
ichthyology, how the sun strikes
so his shadow pushes a certain kind of man
off a woman, and what fills in
between them, though its composition is life,
cuts like salt. I have:
a solitaire deck, a butter knife, a 1964 tie
and two lugged cardboard boxes
where friends' small gifts, the porcelain bird-totem
Tony gave me, the chipped stone dragon Ginnie bought,
are stored against movement
in wrapped dark
so deep away from me, they could be Neolithic.
Light would powder them. And just as the wrist-bones'
waving repeats
up the arm, through the shoulder, and into the thin shell
of chest, until, at 4 A.M., the seismograph
where spine clamps skull graphs
uncontrollable shaking,
                              so
the ear in the pillow
shudders
at the vertical travel —up
centuries of interconnected ancestral remains— of the infinitesimal
creak and sigh
of the continents' undoing.

There was this dog and this man
threw this ball I guess and this dog
went to get it and when he came back
guess what he had in his mouth.

❋

When I left, Syl, remember? I gave you
a hundred balloons, each with its message
slipped in, some crinkled
strips that said *I love you,* some
just with silly
child's jokes. And the child
in me delighted to think you, eyes
winced, hair a wiry-black niagara,
bursting each beneficence out.
                              Now
when the iron asserts itself out of my blood, and is jostled
through the heart in the form of ingots; or the sexual loneliness
seeps through my mattress, and hangs gray semen
stalactites into the dark below the bed; or the watch-face
is set surgically in my chest; or the marsupial
rat in my pocket scents my liver's suds; or the words
in my mouth turn drool; or hurt; or cowardice;
or 4 A.M.;
          I still think
of evening in Elmwood Park, each house
a time capsule
of twentieth-century light through the ages' dimness,
how
one house in its each timber joist
and wood slat decor
is clacking like castanets, and in this hubris I see
it as a ventriloquist's speech
for my hundred blown breaths.

When I was —oh, under
ten— I cried to cousin Bevy about the deaths
breaking the ribbon, like skeleton
racehorses, out of the radio every night.
And she said, she must have been sixteen
then or so, how just because they never
announced the good news, that didn't mean
it didn't happen, it *did*, in fact
too much to announce. And now
child, let me tell you
the same old story
with the same straight face:

*

The stars rise
out of the Earth every night.
There's a face
in the moon to guard our sleeping.
No matter what
the sun always returns.
And a man,
if he'll dig
deep enough for good news, till his nails
strike sparks against bedrock, finds
how memory comforts, how
Tony's palm-sized bird and Ginnie's
sweet Korean monster
can be lifted
into daylight
shaking great clots of night from their shoulders,
burst cages of carbon 14.

*

A bone from the other joke!!!

A mill: water
grinding Earth;
                        a planet,
spinning, endless, as if 4
grandparents slotted in place
made a motor.
                        Like the stars
that were there all along but it needed
something so dark
as death to set
the kings and fabulous beasts in position,
the underearth
                        glows, quick bulbs
of phosphorescence in a ribcage lit
at the pit of a grave as if a city
from air.
                        All along, the father
was the house. And the candles are set in the windows
until we come home. And he keeps
our rooms ready.

❋

The old myths return. And we stand
hands twined on the beach near where the line of lake
and the definition of flagstone
mix —or we stood there
once— —or we'll stand there again— and

the stories are close, in our breathing. Now,
in one held breath, we can see,
along the symbiotic horizon,
the Earth stands still.
                        And the sky,
the punctual flashing night sky, rolls out of the waters.

Look, Syl: our balloons
from the other poem, coming back.

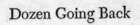

Dozen Going Back

The Food Pyramid
2075

1.

Sun rides the network of protein
in a drop of sweat. The archaeologist
rests a moment along the edge of the works.
All day they've been digging
down —and now, each their respective sips
of water / rum / or cola replenish the huge communal
pouring out. And there —where the scholar
with his sifting-pan sprawls in the shade
of the bulldozer's ton . . . the poles of energy,
raw to refined. The works
itself is still an undefined maw: a bumper
here, an ancient welding-torch there . . . they've
hit an auto plant it looks like, pressed
and crusted in the filth of the last,
the twentieth, century.

2.

Kee-rhist! Twenty years at this dump, boys, and
his stomach predicts the lunch whistle by
twenny sekuns PREEcisely so's you can set
your watch by the rumble. They thunk
down torch, or lug-wrench, the sweat
in the undershirt cools and asserts itself
against the armpits with the pressure of crutches.
Lunch break: now,
neglected, quarter-panels and fenders
swivel in the unplugged dark like slabs of beef
from robot cows, and the huge tin rolling closed
of a door as the last man packs out for BeerTown
touches
off the enormous collision, thud
and clank, between the trunk-lids and roofs, the massive
industrial wind-chimes
energizing air through the auto works.

3.

And a man needs this
after four hours being the flame that marries
metal to metal: hey Rosie, with pickle
n lettuce n mustard to go! N a beer.
N another beer. And he'll bring it back and it's four
more hours' sweat, and here
a fly lights
where a bubble of sugar is breaking the surface of lactase,
where the microscopic greeds of intestinal villi suck,
where it's dark, where the elemental spark
is struck against the pinhead supporting
the food pyramid, a drop of pastrami, dropped
from pastrami to go
with the works.

The Two Poles: *a New Year resolution*
1975

In the arctic, it only needs to snow once
❀

And sorrow is on the land, a static, everywhere,
the photos develop like long-drowned faces
surfacing, weeks later, into the insufficient light,
there is sorrow upon this land, there are
ashcan babies and little difference between being pierced
by a man or by a needle for some women, sorrow
is heavy here, a part of us, affixed, a glance
received in passing on the street is removed
from a heart that night by the ballistics crew, these are
sorrowful times and the subway stations themselves will not do
as symbols for the necessary moaning, sorrow is here
to stay and the arch of a cat's back bridges
the process of understanding grief and connects
something unspeakable registered in its eyes with
its fearful, uncontrollable sphincter, and we
if we could see in the dark a cat sees
would do the same for these are sorrowful times
we live in and die away from, oh I say
sorrow is on the land and a single hair
on the body, somewhere, desires to prickle
with joy and the nervous system
says no, not here, not this one
❀

says the taxi driver, all the way uptown.
The snow behind us is gray and almost ice
with our weight. It's late.
I invite him in, he fits in
well with the man making castanets
of the bamboo slivers driven under his nails,
the man whose betrayal by close associates shines
from the ax-hack deep in his back, the woman
with the riveted breast, the one who orphaned
his testicles so many years ago, all of you,
thank you for making it to my annual Come As You
Would Like To Never Be Party, it's good
that you're here. You're my resolution:
our griefs are immense
❋

and our joys must be commensurate.

The Origin Of Porno
1878; the Muybridge equine series

Studying the horse, we understand
how hard-core followed the invention
of photography. There's a dark compelling
muscle framed by the flanks. There's

a question, an academic question, of at
which point in a leap the female breast
is highest? In the early stopwatched studies,
light slopes down the breasts like a scree. There's

a question of time, there's a sepia
exactitude. The powder erupts:
in the foreground —two lovers / a basket / red wine.
In the back, a clocked thoroughbred sudses.

*Is there ever a moment when all four feet
leave the ground?* And so we invent pornography.

Silk
1700; Eastern Europe

In orthodox *schuls* the women were kept
separate, in a balcony, plain
black dowdy gowns and babushkas. They
didn't count, but hovered

overhead through the service at the edge
of concentration, black-haired,
black-holed, at the back of a prayer, already
unspinning their black hems

for nightfall. The sex-scent Bombykol:
one molecule from the female silk-moth's glands
triggers the male —it will think glass
air in its frenzy. And counting,

17,000 sensory hairs on the male moth's antenna,
300 odor molecules per second, is praying
too, in its own way, a carrying out
of our tally of wonder

to new sums, new levels. And in it,
the ancient lesson —God has been seen contained
in hatsize. A dream: the family's heirloom
black silk *yarmulke* rising

into its component moths and circling
my head, the old domestic
angels. They were there
at the first fast's break, and will be

every morning thereafter, distracting
us from something so small as the heavens
that fit our eyes to something so huge
as what fits fondling.

Puritania
1600

Sparrows were falling. On every one
God's eye, that peacock feather, was pasted.
Today was the day to strop the blades.
There were four seasons; winter,
like winter water, was hard. The first snows
hit like brass studs. One day The Tempter
was in the leek patch, but fire
applied to the tongue of the maid who saw him
drove him out. Melissa Prentiss
had a voice like unto a nightingale.
They smiled, and sang. They could not put
their hands in their pockets. God's eye
was pasted on everyone. Today
was the day to tan the hides. The Deceiver
was seen in the hog trough. Today
was the day to grind the ax. The buckle
functioned, and kept them in. They worked.
Their jewelry was a night
in the stocks. They wore black,
and black. The first snows and God's eye
were black. The buckle framed the prong.
Today was the day to strap the wife
and carve the poultry. The first snows
cut, like saws. God's paste
was cold. One day The Devil's eye
was long, and icy, upon her
in bed. It was hard.
They walked to Los Angeles.
It was hard. They bundled,
and bundled up.

Wire
1595, Italy / (Utah, 1975)

The blood of storm-crazed cattle crusted
rust-colored on the asterisk-prongs of barbed wire . . .
I think of Galileo, battering himself
against the concept of the fixt stars. Surely
now that we can think beyond such boundary,
we can turn to see an old star, a red star, burning

with the odor of a drop of his blood. Out West
they name it like constellations,
pretty: The Upham Snail, The Kelly
Diamond, or the Brinkerhoff Knife, twenty
kinds in one display. A man can climb it
to bring back news of the universe

expanding and contracting to the startled world,
but . . . here he comes, babbling, and sewn
across his palms. An inmate told me once, he had
a recurring vision while working the fields: in
the sun and sweat of the State of Utah Penal Farms
he has sex with a woman who's come

through all that, her body scarred
as a planetarium ceiling. And making love
with her is an entering the sky
beyond where the stars are fixt, and a looking
down to see what's important —the earth,
our breaths— be whole and all wire be suture.

Europe Makes It Through The Plague
1495

with 2 quotes by Hans Zinsser

"From the time of its arrival, the rat spread across Europe
with a speed superior to even that of the white man in the
Americas."

A butterfly over a rat. Or rather
a flag, breeze-borne and bright
as a Monarch, fluttering gaily
at the farthest tip of Spain —above
Columbus's head. His touch breeds
reciprocity; and the spread of dying

Indians *untill theyr Bodies Wch dropt*
by GunnShot or Sworde could Payve
the Swampes and bee a Road
is balanced by one stiff prick
as trading-vessel between the Indies
and Europe: Spain imports *stooles*

little more than Rags of Blood,
&Sores in the Bones as awfull
in size as Eggs & they run Slime:
syphilis, 1495. Make a coat of arms
of the worst of both plagues: a waitress
opens herself for a quick one

two three for a trucker's twenty
last bucks in the can of the latest
eruption of *All-Nite Donut Villas*
westward, like lemmings, to California.
Or simply broider our flag with a rat
beneath a butterfly, *for the Rat gnaws*

the bellies of living swine and in the dawn
we had to slaughter three elephants
for the rats had been at their chained feet
past recovery; and the next day sign
of the Plague on a cheek. In the city, one rat
per man: a fact; they couple determinedly

as humans. "Uninterrupted transmission
from one human to another has led to gradual
mildness of the disease. If mankind could be
kept as thoroughly syphilized in the future
as it has been, another thousand years
might produce a condition of which the host is all

but unconscious." Is that the goal? For
the waitress undoes her netted bun
tonight for her husband, and parts
where it abides, and in her communication
of syphilitic love catches candlelight,
pure and intermittent, on her body's shine

and they love, and both transform themselves
for the future —as the bright-winged English
flutter-by is linguistically warped over
centuries. Trace it in gold thread, a crown
for our rodent, a gleam reprieving the sickened
and sooty. We make it through. We learn to live

with our errors and call them our beauty.

Relics
1300; on pilgrimage: the gist

Here, in azure velvet, the silk-polished hammer,
anvil and stirrup bones set backwards in the ear
of a Bavarian monk, that his brain could transmit
visions of Heaven directly into the atmosphere through
such reversal; the thumb a rebel cenobite axed off
to signify the need for opposition; ascetics' welts;

where went the fat of The Glutton Monk when he starved
one year in penance? if not distilled from the very air
for this lily-scented soap; these are miracles; here,
lest your Bible gather dust, the whisk-broom made
from the beard of a better-known prophet, and bound
with the mourning-band a potentate wore for him; these

are miracles, and if you'll pay for spittle or nail-parings
go elsewhere: I bring you the purple flower of penicillin
shot through a holy man's last infected days,
an anchorite's spilled seed for which a corresponding
number of virgin births are recorded; nothing ordinary,
no layman's optic nerve, though it did move mountains,

rivers, two swart children, and the visible stars up its length.

Village Wizard
1200

Begged by a novice-wizard to display the secret
of his craft, Waziri demonstratively
kept silent.

Asked to perform at the Merchants Bazaar
a feat never seen before, Waziri came
with a dozen coins in his purse and left
with a dozen coins in his purse.

Requested by the husbandless maid to conjure,
Waziri concocted three gifts: a flask of lotion
scented with spice; a beaker of potion
made with grapes; and a potent amulet
wrought with pearl to wear on a necklace
between her breasts when she bared her breasts
to the waxing moon. Even her husband
called it magic.

Paid to recite a spell for sleep, Waziri
began his life story.

Told to foresee the Emperor's future,
Waziri closed his eyes.

Ordered to exorcise evil influence
from the royal heir at his birth,
Waziri cut the umbilical cord.

Commanded on pain of death to provide the impossible
virgin speculum for the Queen, that fabled mage's mirror
so pure, it would have imaged nothing —not its maker,
not the air, and not the darkness— before her face
reflected there: with pity's stare, Waziri, wizard,
wept that tear.

The Children's Crusade For Peace
1100

Far enough away, they were dust motes
wind couldn't detour, wind couldn't cool.
The crows continued to hobble among the dung
in the fields, the town whore
drew open the scarlet drapes
she wore for a skirt, the smithy, the fish cart,
the mother lifting the infant to kiss her
milk in, the rags, the cobbles, the wrens

much as usual in such times: all
aware of how they cast shadows
larger than they were, how if the shadows fit
together just so, it would be night forever.
When we looked again, the dust motes
were children marching through
the village gates: maybe a hundred
with the sound of romping and raillery

sewn in the guarded purses
their tongues were, cached in clamped jaws.
No crow flew out of their path, but watched
the procession of small patched pilgrims
as if a huge wing had been reassembled,
and this was its new anatomy
after passing through a predator's body.
Their faces were soft enough to smile

but didn't, the smile having gone
into marching; to want to march with
was a smiling back. The fisher
let go his cart, and the smithy stopped breathing
his bellows; everybody wanted to be a boy
stepping with such pacific purpose, a mother
nursing her heart out her breast on the left road,
a tart's flapping bodice the flag of the right, and he

off! with lips singing hymns of praise
between one nipple and the other.

Looking Back
1000; a hill in the Mediterranean

1.

He studies the last of the moon divide
across her breasts, the motion of smaller moons:
dust-motes shine with reflected light and set
and rise continually at her nipples. And then,
before she'll wake, he leaves the tent: recent rain
on the horse's forelegs, each bead filling vertically

with new sun. But the man walks for this, leaves the horse
snort and graze. Now, at the hilltop: he faces the rainbow,
mumbles, turns, and from his bared backside shits
out the morning's oblation, then returns to her to watch
her eyes' first flutter and tell her: I've seen a sign He
favors our journey.

2.

In those days God spoke with every lamp the lightning
cracked into a cedar stump, He answered
implorations rising mutely up whatever trachea
formed in the long neck of smoke between the altar-brazier
and stars, and men could point to a raven circle
the wedding-tent twice and outline

a breast each time, the tent its nipple, prophesying good
to come in two's. A racial memory looks back
to that in myth —a paradisal garden, say,
symbolic of pre-agrarian ease— as a single man
looks back fanatically to a better time in his life
until it's stylized, geometric, in his head.

3.

And on a sleepless night, like this night, it
announces itself. A man alone in bed with the traffic
at 2 A.M. the only whisper he's heard all night:
will calm himself, as if belief in the past betokened
well for the future, and force his eyelids to clamp
on a memory: under each lid: a version of one of her breasts.

It's a small renewal of faith, they say at Dachau
even, men would sing the old *schul* songs and the gun
in the mouth punctuate it. Well this isn't
that bad. Just: I miss you. One cheek, awake
with nostalgia, looks back into its eye for a moment
and wets and dries and is a pillar of salt.

The Evolution of Equus
millennia B.C.

". . . the ancestor of our modern-day horse . . ."

Twelve-toed Merychippus grazing Siberia's border grasses,
staring westward with tremulous eyes, becomes a potential
horse. Can't you see him, crossing the now-long-gone land bridge
to Alaska? Kinetic and potential coasts, communing, make
a generator, and sparks fly. Can't you see him at night,
kneeling with exhaustion on the North American plains,

having just completed the isthmus, and by the flash of stars
off his mate's bared teeth and mud-pomaded hooves, now nuzzling
a trail of horse-lipped kisses up her shaggy equine throat?
Or maybe it's too dark to see. Still, in expectation
of your ambassador, my vigilance hangs suspended
in the fixative night like two zeroes in the address

over my door. No word this week; or last. And straining
oval-eyed to see the lump of your swallowing something
warm from mind to crotch, I startle at every postman
bobbing through snow to my house, sure the pulsing
jugulars under his icy scarf declare him your emissary;
and fantasize your smooch lavished over the signature

announcing itself, like the leader of a migratory genus bent
to smack wet thanks on New World soil, as here for good.
So what can I say to the empty mailbox? Last night,
again, a dark so thick it wrapped black spools of thread
about the twiddling thumbs. This morning, a ray
of hope: the sound of a dynamo's chug, and a neck reported

floating, cold but making headway, up the Bering Strait.

For The Time Capsule, 1:   Hymnbook

being a week's-worth of psalms, and a kaddish for the dead,
from the 1970s

Incline thy ear, and come to me.
One generation shall laud thy works to another.

Give us this day, our daily bread.

Song: Stands For

The magpie clawed its calligraphy
into the scarecrow's shoulder. Inside
it molded sun and languid August
heat around its straw, its chest a lax
brick. Inside, the farmer nubbled
his lips at his wife's gorged clitoris,

an effigy. He wanted to take her
in, as she could him, this was his wet
synecdoche of reception. The tumor
in her sex grew, hard as nut. The head
in the den bore real antler but glass
eyes in effigy of death. Outside the scarecrow

sported a necklace of gun, the empty chamber,
that bullet of air —protection
in effigy. The doctor said she was in the pap
on the slide —he often thought of the perils
of Pauline, a woman hanging by her nails over
the glass edge. Inside the calf was total acceptance

of teat, the line between *milk* and *mother* its
first cud. Maternity burned in lactase
in effigy, and it bleated. The circle of green world
hung on the scarecrow's crosshairs, the one star
burning every night through the rifle's bore —an eye
down a microscope's plummet, in

effigy. Inside the doctor zipped and said
benign. Outside a magpie lifted like discus
off the straw shrug. There was grain passed
in crowshit, and wingflap above, an
instant, like one seed's blossoming black
petals and a stamen of orange beak. This

was September, in effigy, harvest,
and the bloom on the edge.

Thou hast sold thy people for a trifle,
Demanding no high price for them.

The Pocket Song

For I have been eating tuna fish
and knotting a tie of tuna fish, pink and casual,
around my swallow, and wearing it down
to the peanut butter bank. For you withdraw
peanut butter from huge consignments
of peanut butter collecting interest, crusted
brown along its sides in the vaults,
and the girl slides it over, and smiles,
for hers is a friendly job and a vulva-pink corsage
of tuna fish on her shoulder. The throat
of a whale is so small an orange
won't fit —surprised? That moon is not
green cheese. The car is screwed open and pumped
fat with gallons of peanut butter, and lovers
tonight in each Chicago alley are cuddling
in *park* while the engine turns like a fryer
in peanut butter, they watch the broken glass
reflect the tuna fish moon. He kisses her: breath
of tuna fish. Whales eat anything, cows
bear a second stomach, an extra waxy vat
of peanut butter up to the rutting bull. The mayor
reputedly piles shoeboxes under his bed with half
the colored people's tuna fish soaking the cardboard
and they're not happy about it, for their cars
also have tanks and what's a child if not a second
stomach, while whitey and his industrial
peanut butter claim another stretch of coast.
Offshore, the whale's jaw is wide and indiscriminate;
what it needs it digests, what won't fit
it pukes, a dozen times a day it has reason to envy
the shark contentedly breaking down porcelain
tuna fish, stomach fluids like lye, uranium
tuna fish, and peanut butter upholstery, foaming peanut butter
fish, gray tuna scales knitting sweaters of pink sweet

34

tuna meat in the midnight waters. To keep us
warm. A cold brown wind this winter. A sharp
tuna snow. We need logs. And mittens. And something
else, the cars are beached in icy ditches like overturned
whales, gasping, heaving it up. And we dig
in our pockets, trying to help, and knowing
all the time what we'll find, a January wind
or a child is whining, stuck in the snow,
poor thing, dead engine, poor starved chihuahua, and we
creak open our wallets to pay
and they say: just peanut butter. tuna fish.

> *Therefore I have cursed what I did not understand,*
> *Therefore I despise myself.*

Song In One Serving

This is the song in which a raccoon turns over
at the side of the page, a tire tread indelibly
catching rain on his belly, and I laugh. In this piece
ankle-bones mean to snap down a chain-gang's length
like a string of firecrackers, and some are meant to let
a chill wind in at their breakage, and some designed to confound
all epoxies. Here, a Pakistani student receives an F
in Comp 101, though the sweat on his forehead phosphors,
though the sweat on his forehead manifests itself
with the corporality of phlegm, and he must be deported;
see him? driving wet-eyed through the downpour,
listen closely to the sound of a small brown paper bag
of bones beneath the wheels: the raccoon. In this tune
nothing's dry, and even the rigid MP rubbered up
against the damp is thinking more of his frilly wife found
in the sergeant's arms than of guarding the base, you can tell
by one yellow drop of adrenalin too much as it trickles
out the eye and makes a cross with his knife-edge line
of mouth, or by my guffaws. Agnes, what you saved
from me at the party after our high school prom is pronged
this morning by a surgeon's spear; too bad. Go home,
need desperately to have your husband say he loves you
anyway, and find a note: he's just found out
about the sergeant, he's leaving you. And Sarge?
is gone to war; this afternoon, inside a song like this,
he ships out for Karachi, Pakistan having bombed
two-thirds of our Eastern coast; the general wipes
thick sweat from his forehead and thinks, before his camel
explodes, how demolition reverses his failing grade
more surely than just repeating the course. Bridges
fall, mutts pee on wooden legs, bullet-holes appear
in the nipples of half the nation's convents; great!
This is the poem in which I exorcise all of my superfluous
hate. Let it dish up gall in another plate.

The seed is no less great than the whole of the field,
And of thy wondrous works will I meditate.

Song: Simple Truths
        after Talarico

Tears are the closest we come
to pearls. This is true.
A day is twenty-four hours long.
I've measured.
12:01 —a jack-knife on the clock
opens, reams out another hour.

What goes up
is futile. Ice melts.
Sleep follows waking. One side
of a bed is always a little less
in the present. These are
the obvious truths.

A hurt
requires a hurt.
The moon is arid. It has
a cycle of thirty days.
Its shine can fill the hands,
heavy, strange as fish-milt.

The life of a one-dollar bill is seventeen months.
There are more basic facts. If you drive
unlit for long enough, down enough
wet streets, somebody
will blink his brights. But, first,
we must like ourselves.

The Babylonians named the testicles
Anu and Hoa. The earth is not round,
it goes as far as the highest xylem: picture
a central hub, with spokes.
Our ability to symbolize
saves us.

More: we're not created equal.
Some of us have been found eating snow,
some with a predilection for pussy.
Still, certain emblems can permeate
the consciousness of entire generations:
snipers, ecology.

It's two to four minutes
between the heart's surrender
and the brain cells' death. This is
true. The facts on the mayfly would stun.
We've learned to find new things beautiful:
the simple curve of a paper clip.

A man lives his life until he dies.
This is proven. My cornea breaks the sun.
And when I pass a funeral parlor,
hearse, cemetery
or ambulance: I hold my breath.
I won't breathe it in.

Therefore thus saith Yahweh:
"If thou utter what is precious, and not
What is worthless,
Thou shalt be as my mouth."

The Formula For The Poem

There's a woman you've fucked. She's folded
into so many curves, complacently, like a bolt
of cream muslin half-undone on the couch. Or
sometimes, just to soften the razor-edge
accuracy of your initials carved in the linseed finish,
there's a woman, quasar eyes and plum-tits,
you haven't fucked. But the point is
she's in a room, turning slowly gray and distant
as a brain cell that won't yield its secret
fully, and a sadness passes overhead, maybe
a line of geese in the steel sky of November is
to your window what a thread is to the needle's eye
and the name being stitched is red,
in cream muslin, and closes like a wound.

You can add you've been walking, your legs
knee-high in the undulations of autumn leaves like
the upthrust arms of a drowning man and your face
is the word he's shouting. There's your father's hand
like a perched bird on your shoulder; it's been banded
with a ring, like any wild flyer, that shows how far
its nest is. This is the past, your recognition
of the past. And when the clouds break, there's a pull
on you, toward that rift in the claret air, as if
the bullet were forcep'ed out of its wound, the one
we mentioned earlier. This is the future. And
this is the formula, and it can be followed
easily enough. Let the drowning man sink with the bullet. Sing
with your scars. Let the poem darken the better for stars.

Three visions art wondrous overmuch to me;
   Four pass beyond understanding:
The way of an eagle in the sky,
   The way of a serpent on the rock,
The way of a ship on the high seas
   And the way of a man with a maiden.

Love Song In Three Movements:
   Entomology / Astrology / Philology

/Sugar Rises   /for the times

The sci-fi story about the rhinoceros
ants disassembling Kenosha in fiendish glee:

bullshit. Physiological fact is an ant that size
can't lift an eyelid. There's just this everyday picnic

intruder absconding with constellations of sugar
grains, which today, April 1975, cost three times more

than last year —inflation,
what makes things, ants, us

all, too big for proper handling. Here, in the countryside
warmth, science fiction solar-years astound but

what astonishes more is what fits
between lips, the sugary give of a nipple, or what

economy in the way your blue-gray eyes hold
and double the sun. The strength

is *in* the smallness, in
bearing the sweetness no matter the cost.

/Horoscope: Jan 21–Feb 19   /for the self

Say the father's felt it. Somewhere
in the mother's a cluster
of stars. We call it *nova*, a
birth, they hang from one black bellynerve
like chandelier, and you're born.
There's one stink but twelve signs. Yours,

say, Aquarius. It was hand over hand,
for a breech-baby, down the umbilicus. If
a man stashed you in a woman, if her waters
broke because that was the constellation, this
is what we assume: the navel a lock
and star-motif the combination. Yours,

say, the bearer's tipped urn in '48. And
so, say, this is the proof of women as a mystery
that can be entered. Often, touching the flush
in their skin was other-worldly. This is
because of the birth-thread, the connection. Some
men, yes women too, consult it. Yours

says Today check business assets, Today
romance is a penetration, Today happy
birthday. The string twangs. Some, the dogs
of us, are walked on those leashes.
Some hang. And some are
climbing that rope. You, yours.

/Synecdoche: A Survey   /*for the woman*

As in Shakespeare, at The Globe, that sweated
actor applauding the wedding march stands
for a townfull. *He knew the Orient Word and Economy*

of my hand inside you, itself
now, rooting
a perfect bonsai.

Thou didst afflict the peoples,
But then thou did set them free.

Toward Survival, A Song In Triptych:
       Yesterday / Today / Tomorrow

/John & The Lusitania

There are no bees at a harbor.
They know, the salt air
is no perfume. It cuts copper. You cough.
It cuts the copper in the blood.

You cough. The turbot know,
and fat themselves like insulated wire.
But copper's snipped everyday.
Every day a message doesn't get through.

Rats know in their whiskers, bees in their legs.
A pinhole
could let the ocean in, given time.
Given time, the page will mulch.

And there, with the lungs
puffed up and pumping, some huge conveyance
the shape of a human chest
is sailing away from you.

It's your health, Keats. Its one rat
abandons it.

The inefficiency of paddling a canoe
with a tennis racket:
ideal. And so we remain, and our loves
and intents remain, in place on the pond-top,
allowing the time to study detail: this
water-spider stepping a gradual mandala
into the surface, how biography's composed
of careful fact as is green
accumulated in pointillism of blue and yellow and so
we arrive at the color of ponds: still, algaeic water.

But a certain sweep
of a certain oar, as in a stroke, almost swath,
of green across a Van Gogh pond, is fierce
and general, and propels. And at the sign of its being
needed —say, a cry from the elderberries
onshore, or a cloud so charged it lusts to light
down your bones— you'll paddle
this way, hard, efficient, with your hand
if the oar's gone, your tongue, your prick
could row and the scenery flash past without nuance.

And it works. This careful structure I've made,
the pond, the boat —I'm talking about
right now. Suppose the things you've said
built up in me like a delta
on which henbane grows; or the wail
in the cradle starts, or the ax that carved
last evening's headline is at our door. This is
not the time for leisure, and we learn to think
in quick bold strokes: Van Gogh:
his eye was good and his ear came off.

/List For The Capsule

The mower's swathed.
In May breeze whatever
chancy grasses escaped the blade
do their hula. Today, I'm Gulliver
of the ants, let them scale
this monolith, their grains cupboarded
between my toes, their cairn of eggs in my pinna.
Today: a quart of skim milk. Today:
forsythia. Let this day be recorded
in the sweet wake of the reaper, and go

in the time capsule. May 7, 1975. Today,
a letter: they pincered the lump
from Aunt Sally's neck, that
dangerous raisin. It floats
in its vial, black
and furled as the brain of a soldier-ant
jawing its saws sharp. And I'm
on capsules myself, for the dark jar of lard
that's my heart. Today
the milk better be skimmed, no rich chawing
teat-fat to clog me. Today
the sun's thread. My eyes
two brown buttons. Tomorrow,

maybe, they'll shovel up
some life like mine from between its wrack
for a 30th-century needle fine
enough to play the pressed music
in brain-grooves. And then let the lyrics be
how while the oceans were drying
to chancroid pocks; the gun muzzles
periscoped up the world's jiggling asses;
the leech
applied to the conscience bloated
enemabag-grotesque —it was

okay, sometimes, forsythia shook flame
from its pigment, the day danced. It's
true, a capsule in the cornerstone
of a new Chicago superstructure —our civilization
on microfilm, in models. And let this
listing be scrolled: We hoped for the best,
We tried big. Let them knife up
that bundle in consultation and nod ah
yes, benign. A benign one.

kaddish

The Whole Picture: Morris Gilman, Uncle; 1912–1969; I See Him

For the majority of his stay on Earth —in fact up to only the last
two or three hundred years— man has conceived of his chronology
as cyclic: the rhythm of the seasons; the alternation of day/night,
sleeping/waking; the ritual slaughter of the regent to assure next
year's crops; even Neanderthal burials, with their grave-objects in-
dicating belief in future resumption of daily function, their impli-
cation of placing-back-in-the-womb. Time was rotund.

In winter: a pure, bare bush; as if the convolutions
pristinely, without the brain. I pass it suffering
snow, sometimes draped like a *shiva* mirror
with snow, forgotten. If this is the mesh the lawn
thinks with, it's comatose by the 1st of the year.

❋

A dream: Neanderthaloid male, female,
child, dancing a ring —what sociology terms the family
nuclear unit. And so they become a physics
diagram of the atom: sub-particles bonded
and circling —a kind, everywhere, of perpetual music.

❋

He was an engineer, he puttered. I see him:
cameras, gadgets that sparked. I picture
him soldering a model, hand-sized, of the
north-south magnetic axis and its
east-to-west crossbar of sun shot home.

It is with the Crucifixion —an event the central doctrine of which declared it to be unique in time, not subject to repetition— that the idea of time as a linear movement, and not a cyclic one, initiates. The course of Western culture reinforced this: the credo that "time is money" and thus time lost can never be banked away; the forward thrust espoused by Darwinian evolution; the recent Big Bang theory of an ever-expanding universe —all substantiated our current belief in chronology as a straight line.

He tinkered. He prodded. I picture. I
see him lifting his small metal cross of the planet's
four directions, and /instructive lesson/ with
one pennyweight nail driving the thimble-sized
jew deep into its center.

✽

For when you sit *shiva* they bring what's sweet, small
wickerboxes of oranges flown from half-around the world
this winter, to soften your loss. But you sit on slivered
orange-crates, a symbolic, bearable, agony; and linen
over the mirror lest the face of the dead confront you.

✽

*A dream: an ape peeks from over each
one of the Saviour's shoulders, then scampers along one
outstretched arm to its ominous
plank-edge; one drops a stone; one, a feather; chanting
Thirty-two-thirty-two-feet-feet-per-second.*

The Russian poet Samuel Marshak, in London, before 1914, stopped
a man on the street and in his broken English asked, "Please, what
is time?" The man, surprised, replied, "But that's a philosophical
question." Indeed, it is. And much of our time-sense is subjective.
As late as mid-century, every Japanese claimed the same birth-date:
the New Year, when time regenerated and the cosmos was born
anew. The attitude waits, for our partaking.

A dream: the Passover table. We're seated
around it, what Western Art calls the
last supper; when, starting near Uncle Morrie,
the room is suddenly rolled up into Eastern Art: a
Japanese scroll; the family, round as a clockface.

*

He plumbed. He reasoned. In my picture
I see him saying the arms of the cross-shape are no
stopped watch. And he fashions shining wire
circles around it —a gyroscope. The
Earth, he announces; forever; in balance.

*

And: there's no disconnection, though the gap be
dry blank paper, what ancient Japanese art terms "flying
white," used for the snowy parts, though it be
all winter. May 1st: and green is being drawn
up the roots, the bush: lush; the bush having remembered.

Letter To Tony

suitable for presentation as a gift

On August 23 gas-masked workmen spent two days
cleaning out a three-bedroom apartment that its resi-
dents turned into a garbage dump with two-feet deep
human excrement . . . Cleghorn told authorities the
apartment's condition resulted from "personal trag-
edy."

—The Chicago *Daily News*

Over the date palms:
Over the preening geese mopping night from the river:
Over the tax-magistrate's stacks of cowskin:
Over the lotus flower:
Over the lion dressed in a Feather of Truth:

> *it's everywhere: for it jewels the land*
> *for it studs the land like copper*

Over the temple:
Over the blood-crusted gutting knives:
Over the basalt coffin, over its eviscerated cat:
Over baskets of eggs, over wooden pillows:
Over the winking penis of Thoth:

> *it's warm; for it falls*
> *in the shape of its body*

Over the rouge block of granite:
Over the gauzy roomful of undulating breasts:
Over vultures:
Over a wheel of vultures, over its fixed centerpoint: a dead bull:
Over Hathor the Cow, udder-suckling the dead:

> *it's life-engendering; for it nurtures*
> *seeds, for green turns toward it*

Khepri rises, He Who Comes Into Existence:
Khepri the scarab beetle:
Khepri-done-in-blue-glaze-on-our-women's-bosoms:
Khepri: dawn in our fields, rolling his lump of dung,
The sun, through what we call Sky over what we call The World

according to ancient Egypt, Tony.
A ball of shit when you wake.
This is a letter because I know
Sharon's left you. I know
what that's like, how she'd been the bed's
other side for so long, for such peace: your faces made the two
    pillows
a coin to buy sleep with, and now
here's your only ha'pence: a man
face down in the sheets, with no
obverse. It's how we pay
for mistakes. I know, now
your hands, without her breasts, want to fold
on all fours, like herbivores
spent in chill. And it gets cold
in Salt Lake City, I know, the sands about it
give up heat each night with the zealous, ascetic will
of religious conversion —no cow kneels there
but for the leaden presence of God, I've seen Him
force a girl to hands and knees and the red, sore saddlemarks
pressed in backflesh in the shape
of the Temple floorplan, it's
a bad place to be lonely. Tony, I know, last year
when I lived in Salt Lake with you and Sharon, before
I slid East, when we taught
at the U there, before
the date of your marriage's minting was rubbed, by their too
much commerce, off Sharon's eyes —when
we encouraged careful words
for a living: I saved
this scrap of student error —in retrospect strangely, unfortunately,
prophetic: *Once you start to cook it on a too hot burner
the pieces will dislove.*
❋

Oh they have electric mixers
Oh they have hot-plates
Oh they have a machine
That spins blood
Until it separates

❋

I'm writing to tell you . . . The week of my flying
out, The Salt Lake Museum of Fine Arts imported an Ancient
   Egypt Exhibit,
at home
in the harsh, contextual sands of Utah,
remember? Mural: a flock of heron, you and Sharon
circling their movement instinctively
in imitative grace: fluctuating
relative position but maintaining the sense of the whole,
the connection. That was
then. And there were the stares of the hawk-lidded gods,
and the small things: handmirrors, gameboards, shell combs. And
one dung-beetle, an inch
glazed blue —though then our world wasn't dark enough
to see it burn, almost bunsen blue, with the fervor
of its mission. Now I know. And
now I see you trying to fragment together your life
like an Egyptologist faced with pyramidal sherds
and the tweezers. I know, by braille I've read the motto
struck on his pouch's last coin: *Most people, after a certain age*
                              don't cry. They just live
                              that little bit shorter I know
because   Never mind
                              because. I know

the desperate synecdoche
of trying to lose yourself, from yourself, in all of your filling
a series of undomesticated, evanescent pussies; the flag-panties,
each night's new color, run up your life's thin line
in a code for distress.

Moreover, the characteristic odor of human feces is caused
       principally by the products of bacterial action;
              these vary from one person to another,
                     depending on each person's
                            colonic bacterial
                                 flora

Face it . . . unfamiliar
redolence in the morning bowl. Now the whiff of a stranger's
species of the dark, brown rose.

You wrote *were destitute*   *got arrested*   *frigid*
        Everything I was   *dependent on my having Sharon*
        my value   *my earlier mole-like existence*
You wrote *vicious circle*   *a worthless shithook*
You wrote *a turd*   *I feel like*   *very*   *vile*

I know.
But just because
the threadholes in the button darken, threaten to snap
the last of our functioning strands; just because
of the accidental anagrams: live / evil / vile; just
because the taste in the mouth, and the blood in the eye,
each morning are one, and the same, and the season's
last chill flake digs all six blizzard-sharpened points in flesh
with crablouse tenacity; or,
oiled black, the six bulletslots of a handgun revolve
about the sky for our only star of david; just because
of the hole in the sack, the burnhole,
the jaw of the female mantis, just because
it's that low, and that rejected: we *mustn't,* conjuring
all the pejorative, unsubstantiated
connotations of its mythologies, strain
our face muscles into their slandering masks
and spit out, for our summaries, as if the word
itself were a crime to the taste buds: *shit.*
I'm writing to tell you

Australia

breaks low, but cragged, from green sea,
like a dolphin spine on the waters. *The coves*
were examined with all possible expedition.
I fixd on one that had the best spring of water,
Wch I honoured with the name of Sydney. January,
1788: some lips, like the last cut provisions, cake
in brine. *The gale apprd tremendous but*
our Spirits, albeit of a miserable set of convicts
in want of cloaths & every convenience,
were not flagged. Land burst like meridian
Splendour on a blind man & the ship
with English colours flying & much clamour
glides in between the heads of the harbour.
To fowles that greet our Landing, of paradisal
plumage, as Laurikeats, Parrokeats, Cock(atoos)
we bring 5 cows, 3 bulls, 7 horses,
44 sheep. The first colony, Botany Bay.
Business now sat on every brow . . . a party
cutting down the woods . . . setting a smithy's forge
. . . dragging stone . . . but we are fixed & Confusion
gave place to System. Excepting a slight
diarrhoea, & volleys of musketry fired,
we were Strangers that Even to anything
but the utmost peace & good chear & so soon
as this can dream our encampment
flourishing, & us the initial Thrust
of a massive movement, Settlers, Adventurers
all along these gentle ascents. The grass is long
& luxuriant, one Skate struck & hauled in
weighed 336 Pounds, & there is a wild Spinage
here, & oxen & sheep will increase.

Mass Movements

Peristaltic waves of the type seen in the
small intestine do not occur in the colon.
Instead, another type of movement, called
mass movements, propels the fecal con-
tents toward the anus. When it has forced
a mass of feces into the rectum, the desire
for defecation is felt.

colon
izing

Tony, 1975:
39 million bovines let
300 million(!) dung pads a day
on Australia: a fact
and a problem. 5 cows
         2 bulls
         7 horses
and no dung beetles
to undo the day's weight of patties.

for the lift of a cowtail trips their switch
for the cowfart homes their radar
for the steaming cake is true north
for their sight is their smell; their smell, their orientation

". . . without scarabs, pads may lay unchanged for years"
". . . may be putting out of service 6 million acres of pastureland
   annually"
". . . a zone of rank, inedible herbage"
". . . thriving insect pests, except for the service of the dung beetle"

for the meister-jeweler carats the gem with one blow
for the cave is hollowed in rock by the Navajo
for they have carved millennia, and will forever carve thus
for they roll their balls like Sisyphus

Beshatted Australian scientists'
remedy: *Heliocopris dilloni*, rhinoceroid
dung beetles, square, and relentless,
as tanks. The human hand cannot cage them:
they break out. The giant Australian toad
cannot kill them: they break out. Swallowed, they burst
the toad's stomach wall.
                They roll dung
to the size of croquet balls.

for they sow the land, for the turd is their silo
for feces is their hatchery, and their hope
for they are Khepri: life, the self-generating sun
for their seed, as well as their day, is well spent

for love has pitched its palace
in the place of excrement
                                        —Yeats

You wrote *uncontrollable fit of tears*
You wrote *shit on me*   *violent ends*   *masochistic*

The night is as cold as its onan-semen.
I'm writing to tell you

even now, where the alleycat is cantor
and the moon bends to drink
from the sewerage ditch, even now
at the mating of prick and palm with the little rabbi
beer-on-the-breath presiding, here
where exhalation falls on the razor halved
like a damp loaf of bread, now
in the hour of thought like a lovelorn
leaping, to death, off its synapse, here
where the cheese sweats, now
at the crotch's *yahrtzeit* candle, the
dead, the dying, here the placebo
pulse in the wrist, now
the gnawbones the stinklards the gutpastes the dregs
*

the dung-bugs are tunneling
out from the woodwork
to make something fruitful
*

from what a life wastes.

/Now 1 coin, 2 faces/
/Australian science
Egyptian faith/
/beetleback
beetlebelly/

Oh, sure: the stench; the taint of decay. But
   the sweetreeking, celebratory, beneficent
canon of coprophilia!: Coyote
   the Trickster, "primordial shit-thrower, product
of a profound & comic imagination —god,
   man & animal at once" (Rothenberg) —for the Nez Percé,
Coyote fights Shit-Man (loses: pee.yew!) or gulps
   shit-berries: scrambling a tall tree can't top him
safe above his growing diarrhetic heap: satisfies
   our bent needs, therapeutic. As Martin Luther
flings ordure to drive the Devil hence. As chanting
   ancient Israel offers up bulldung on Yahweh's
cosmic table: a cleansing. A healthy
   belching it forth: the connoisseur of cursing,
Rabelais' Gargantua ("A turd for him.
   I wish your bum-gut falls out.") and his lavish
liturgy of sixty-three tries ("from parsley
   to pigeons") at finding the perfect rump-wipe:
"the neck of a goose." Our most-exalted
   in, or into, our most overlooked. As in
the folk-motif, widespread, of dreaming buried
   treasure x'ed out on a bowel-map (see
Legman, *The Horn Book,* p. 186). As the Indians'
   holy piling of cow-pies. As orthodox
alchemy procedure: transmutation of basest matter
   to spirit. Or, as in more
embodied magic, the dollop of dung
   as aphrodisiac: one witch (Masters, *Eros and Evil*)
mixes her feces in four abbots' gruel: three die
   at the zeal of copulation, one goes blather-mad
("that each had eaten a considerable portion
   of her bowels, showing the judges how much by marking
off a place on her arm"). The ubiquity of,
   the revelry in, gut-filth! Even rabbits: *silflay hraka,*

"eat shit" in lapine language, according to Adams
   in *Watership Down*. As in FBI files: fact: ⅓
of all housebreakers, terrified, void
   on the scene of the crime. As in scholarly dissertation:
Evolutionary Trends Among Mollusc Faecal Pellets. As
   if the visual symbol of all our aspiration: the fungus
Philobolus grows on dung, builds fluid pressure, shoots
   its sporangium eight feet high: a gross, and grandiloquent,
fountain. As —or *ass,*
   or *arse,* the Greek *orrhos*— more to the pungent point
than any of these, the passage
   —as in *literary section,* or *journey,*
or *defecation*— gracing Aristophanes:

But why on earth have you saddled a beetle,
father, for your ride at the gods?

/For he is the only living winged creature,
as Aesop tells us, to have climbed such a height.

But shouldn't you have bridled Pegasus,
more fit a steed for the Pantheon?

/No, for then I should have needed double rations.
But now, whatever food I consume will in one shape
or another serve two. Ha—! Now! Leap up now, heavenward,
my carriage, my punt, my rising prayer, my gardendragon!

                    (*Exeunt*

Joseph Campbell, quote: One system of imprints that can be assumed to be universal in the development of the mentality of the infant is that deriving from its fascination with its own excrement, which becomes emphatic at the age of about two and a half. For the child, at this period of its life, defecation is experienced as a creative act and its own excrement as a thing of value, suitable for presentation as a gift . . .

The Salt Lake Museum of Fine Arts: Ancient Egypt
in the harsh, contextual sands of Utah,
remember?

. . . In societies in which this pattern of interest and action is regarded as unattractive, a socially determined organization of response is imposed sharply and absolutely, the spontaneous interest and evaluations of the earlier period of the child's thought being even strictly repressed. But they cannot be erased. They remain as subordinated, written-over imprints: forbidden images, apt on occasion, or under one disguise or another, to reassert their force: the arts.

the hawk-lidded gods / Case 1. *Horus, divine sun-hawk. Diorite*
                              From Giza. Old Kingdom, IVth
                              Dynasty.

survives in our adult interest in painting

handmirrors / Case 6. *Cosmetic mirror, inlaid bronze.*
                     From the tomb of
                     Tuthmosis IV.

smearing of all kinds, sculpture, and architecture

gameboards / Case 10. *Wood board, with bronze pieces.*
                     Note sun-ray motif.

the value of the sculptor's marble and clay

shell combs / Case 13. *Ass't toilet articles. Shell*
                     with gold and onyx.

and of the materials of the painter

one dung-beetle   /   Case 27. *Scarab pendant. Of*
glazed faience.
Ca. 1900 B.C.

derived from the bowels of the earth

these artworks have survived intact from
these artifacts cite the heritage of a

Legacy
❀
passed
❀
down to us
❀
These stones
❀
These jewels
❀
These

coprolites:

the museum of lace mantillas,
crusted sacrifice altars, pronged dildoes, crushed
dolls' heads, exploding snowflakes,
spun stars, and crystal chandeliers

of pollen

under the microscope. Tony:
cattail pollen, wild sorghum,
hackberry, mesquite, pine, yucca, tulip
locked
preservatively in these
dark cases.

This is the archaeologist
Scarabaeus sacer digging for treasure: gold
maize, returned
from the boomerang

bends of the body. These are
the long halls of history, this is
what it's willed us

despite the rage
to abort, and deplete, and dim, and vandalize,
and contracept:

This art: these smear-gifts renewed at every birth.
And this seed.

The promise kept.

You wrote
We kept getting fatter and uglier . . . arguments . . . enormous
   perverse
need . . . substituting for a life.

And now, forgetting the poem, I'd simply like
to write back to you
to make a gift of part of a letter, I think
something true, received from Phil Dacey
the same week as yours

Deaths in the Fall have meant a lot to me. In 72 it was the suicide
of a colleague at the college. In 73 it was a student of mine, a
boyish boy, in a car accident. He wasn't driving. Last Fall it was
my aunt, who jumped from the 9th floor of her apartment building.
The deaths stay with me. I walk around charmed, the recipient, the
continuous recipient, of a gift. I do things, as a result, I would not
have done five years ago. The days of my life seem more and more
like celebrations.

Tony, if you go back to the poem,
accept it,
what editors call
Goldbarth's crap, as literal
as possible
a cross-pollination between friends.

What if my face blazed here,
in New York, and yours assimilating
Salt Lake City . . . The child's penny
we live on, you and I, that copper taste
of blood in our mouths, that rusty cameo
circling our heads minted into the world's
cheapest unit . . . the coin

would only have to be that much
larger, transcontinental, it's holding
us together even now, one face
amoebic with grief in Utah, one scavenging
every cairn of droppings in the East . . . we're connected, believe
me, no matter how different the shined sides we stare from:
two men like us will always walk the rim.

*

This: the Other. The
marriage partner; the grandfather's
cemeterial bones spreading under your feet
for your shadow; the hemisphere in,
or not in, sun at the moment; the
twin, the bloom's root, the dream-life, the
two poles, the sex-pulls, the mind and its brain-meat, and

Tony my friend. Tony
my brother. The dark side
of the moon, my Down
Under, this redolent cast
of my inside
shit daily, my
Tony, the Australia of me.

Morning. The dung-bug
is claiming something
so huge, so terrifying,
as distance
and rolling it
into comprehensible units:
the sun's up.
                    The seed's
passed, to pasture.

Tony
I write you a letter.

Tony
Sometimes it's shit
Sometimes night-soil

For The Time Capsule, 2:   Documentation

being some rites, and some wrongs, from the 1970s

. . . so that the testimony of each is important, if we are to understand the age: both the general, inclusive defining of Man's place in the Cosmos; and the individual voice, with the love-glow and hate-sweat of its daily making do.

The Chariots / The Gods

1.
A's Song Through The Centuries

Ty-ty-ty-ty,
A cave came down.
Ty-ty-ty-ty,
A cave came down
With like-us in.

A pyramid descended.
A pyramid in the sky
Descended. Thou hast
Messengers amidst us, here, half-way
Between our stars and our buried.

The shine-condor landed,
Yes! Of-another-tribe walked out,
Yes! They held up bowls to their eyes,
Yes! The bowls made flash, our spirits
Are reflected in their waters. Yes.

2.
/ Reports

/ reports their activities
include digging, making
aggressive action among themselves,
marking territory. He posits
they may be our insides-out

as indicated by their damp-palmed stroking
our snouts, or their kilnwork's accenting
our manes, while they have clearly not seen
within, how our brains are ethereal
gray clouds over sparse landscape

and: their own inverted
lupine, canine, breaks barely forth —insignias
of hair at their sex, or a female
squatting: the animal streams out
gold into humus, ivory into the suckled's lips.

3.
The Lecture

There are stories of angels. Well
astronauts fly. And this is more
reasonable than, say, two pinions
of breath in the lungs, or the infant's skull
fusing closed in a giving off nimbus.

Of course the Red Sea split! Do you think
atomic power, if it could flatten
Hiroshima, couldn't comb
back water? This would explain the
schisms in the Bible.

Spiders walk water. You can see
the principle. "It burned but was not consumed."
"It rained blood." We're thinking
adults here. Use logic. Do I have to explain how
it can rain blood.

4.
The Sermon

There is a story in which a scientist
X-rayed the sky, and what
he found was not celestial bones
but a plate showing nothing —nothing,
that is, cut out to the size of the plate.

If this is the plate we passed
around at the service's end, your coins
would fall forever into the sky
and finally be assured of buying
a word for you at The Ear Of Ears.

But all we pass is a hat. And what we ask
is your coins anyway, and the faith
in a hat's implying
a skull. This is the theory
of god, and archaeology.

5.
Goldbarth Writes A Letter

Ellen: you said there were *bodhisattvas,*
Japanese seraphim. In a land
where writing is fine as red brambles
of capillary in the eyelids:
maybe. I believe it may be.

I believe there are explanations. And if
the angel who turned Lot's wife
salt was a Ph.D. in saline physics,
that's one way. I hope we never have reason
to be sorry when we're looking back.

But if we do turn around, and know her
cutting taste, we mustn't forget
the eyelids. Two wings
are all a world needs,
uplifted in its praise every morning.

The Errors
Central YMCA Community College

1.
When your sad the whole world seams wrong.

You've raised your hands like treasure divers surfacing from the
   gray
bends of the brain with pearls
of miscomprehension, so many breast-pins engraved
with wrong dates. But I want to show you something: these
are the hands that nuzzled a woman's photo and now she wears
his thumbprint for her face; this, the thumb
sucked as if a man would hitch
toward infancy —thumbs
opposed the fingers, invented hammers, built, his
contributed tool was the wrecking-ball
socketed to his wrist; and her birthday poem, the light typed touch
that could have quieted trembling: in these hands *subtle* warped
to *bustle* till the years fell. And now I place them,
palms up, wrong
five-legged beasts with their underbellies exposed, on the desk
for you who have told me, in your own broken wedding
of English and your birthtongue, how *the U.S. sends tanks
and your welcome,* how *the baby hasd no father so
her fren gots a hanger give her a abortcher* —I
know, I grade your papers, the difference between the alphabet
and inkstains leaks from your pens every day thin
as thought. And these, my own
botched lines, the ones in the palmistry handbook
under *Incorrigible,* ask for grading too. So I give them
to you, tonight, the poem
for the Spanish chick who wrote about her first two weeks
in America: a rape on the bus and the driver's La Brea-black
   adam's apple
spit on a knife, said they'd also scooped her purse, said the landlord
opened her one trunk of clothes to the rain. We laughed.
Said she'd come on an errplane.

2.

An adult does have controll of the lifes of young people to a certain extinct.

So we whimper, and our buttocks whipped
by their own blue nerves; how efficient, penitents born with
    congenital
lash. And this is the self-inflicted confession, or its next step,
expiation: I've been wrong
with you, as a lit window too high up
can be wrong and the flocks mistake something that thin, glass,
for dimension. Often you thought this pleased me, these dead birds,
    but
that was no pillow. And for whole nights there has been no place
for my head. If, then, in my sleeplessness, I mocked your sentences,
awkward, and never to take flight, the laughable
dodos in the evolution of prose, you'll forgive my forgetting what
those constructs meant to you, or your pointing out the *pengwin
& orstirch don't fly neither Mr. Goldbart but could beat
your God Damm lark to a pulp.* And you've
been wrong with me. This expectation, that I would clone myself
whole in the lives of each of you . . . In the cliché "thirst for
    knowledge" I
was the reservoir you would faucet at whim. Why is that a too
cute metaphor? What's a cliché? You, the girl in the back
I thought of eleven lines above at the mention of *nights,* and *pillow,*
aren't you listening? Isn't now the time for real
colloquy, here: and I'm beginning with this, my own list of tics
and overexposures, and now it's your turn. For I've seen the
    hound's teeth
working in the gosling's throat, and an infant whose asshole was
    given
to thalidomide and it shit out its mouth . . . and what we think
are errors: belong, and repeat, motifs we wake in the night and
sweat at. And if I invited you over? here, to my house, for the last
    class,
and we swept glass fragments up from around the old, avian
misdirection, and strung them for necklaces. Oh, sure, there's rich
perfect glass: that's lucidity. But here, these chips of cheap sheeting
    of ours:
how the light, when we tilt right, goes rainbow in the flaws.

3.
The tasted of it is to enjoy flesh smell fluit.

A friend writes: KAYAK took his poem, and printed the line "thin
    dresses"
tin dresses, says "my surrealist affiliations only go
so far." I counter with BACK DOOR's prestidigitating my "rabbi"
rabbit. We could war all day, lugging ever larger pyramids of typos
to our howitzers, and never lose the joy of computing injustices.
    Yes, there are
wrongs, miscalculations, for weeping; 'natch: such deprivations
as the insomniac's dream, the mermaid's hymen; even now, the
    small print
in the litigation harbors such malevolences as could raze a house's
    foundations
with their pincers; even now, aren't I the man
who tried to dance in the space between the grains
of a pour of salt; the husband in the coffin doesn't blink,
it's the widow's blurring of vision; that's no silver spoon
in the newborn mouth, it's his eyes spilling silver nitrate . . . But
I've lived errors that, like synesthesia —flesh fruit—, are fortuitous
mismatching and, in the burst breath of a spoonerism, *crime of*
    passion calmed
to *prime of caution,* and we all survived. An error is: nails sleeping
    on a bed
of man —but some have made a religion of that
reversal, daily walk in Jesus' grace. There are insides-out
illuminating our waking, worlds where milk's skimmed off
the top and the bucket of cream gleams like ivory. My friend
M., result of a pin-riddled rubber; my parents, together
26 years from the day they blundered one inch in
each other at Humboldt Park Lagoon; there are accidents
we bless, there are rabbits ordained to bless them, and some
couplings unsymmetrical as a-man-and-a-woman we call
love and writhe with the lack of. It's that
kind of error I wish you, my students, my timid women lifting
suds-white ankles out of tin dresses, my composition assignment, a
    guy
says Columbus opened up a whole new world. For trade. Says
he set sail for the undies.

4.
Being togeter with you are woundefill.

Columbus wakes, with incisive, atlantic, tears in his eyes: *wrong
wrong, no Cathay!* Don't cry, Christopho. I'm here, New
York, writing this and reading Glyn Daniel's *Prehistory,* let us be
   yours
in vindication. He tales how a hare breaks
for cover, the hound follows baying into the lost labyrinthine
   passages
under the Dordogne hills, and when he's finally retrieved
by the ears up a fault in rock, four schoolboys have bumbled
onto the leaping russet cows of Lascaux. Felicitous wrong
turn. There are errors to let the light in, listen: earlier someone
goofed —errplane— and we laughed, a student wrote once how
"they laufed at me, so hard, they were in statues." I think
his word misuse is true —the stiffening, muffling
effects of derision. Combating that, "the prehistorian
witnesses how it is cutlery *sherds* and statuary *fragments,* the
mishaps of daily making do, that endure
when even philosophy, say, or linguistics perish. The noblest
   cultures
shape themselves about the remains of their rubbish chutes." The
   breakage
that tells. The history of our worlds, written
in erasure. Isn't this the one thing
we, all, want to learn: that mistake between us
so breakable, if ever it cracks we'll be married as true
as a kidney transplant —perfect hugging forever . . . Now class
come pillowed around my table, the final exam
tonight is to butcher good taste,
and sentences. Let's try. Let's trust
in our fuckups —that rich, embarrassing trove, and let's
say, *really say,* something indestructible out of groan and clamor,
and we will meat for a hurt
to hurt talk, and with our cleaverest words
eschew the fat.

Dozen Dream Voices

Five Grumbles
                    from the song-poems of François Mouton

The Forswearing Of Women

You roisterers with your codpieces full
as new wineskins, on your tooting way
to the darker entrance in the dark doorway,
drop off a book or two at my place,
some scholarly tome on yellowed vellum
uncared-for under its dust like a beggar's grave,
for I will become a doctor, treating those men
frostbitten by coy looks, flamed by unwashed cunts,
and never again think of a pink thigh —no,
no, get that thing out of my little song!

There are volumes done in leather fit for a cuirass,
on anything possible—the comparative lengths
of moles' whiskers, why the stars do not burn
holes in the night sky, how to count
the sands of the beach on your fingertips.
And I will study these in a solitary light,
with thoughts turning in my head like well-oiled axles
until I drop, like a bookmark, in sleep
—and will wake in the morning reddened by
the antiquated pressure of pince-nez!

The Curse On Collectors

Bagh! Why do they pester me, these debt-hounds,
these ones who suckled at two swollen money-pouches?
Do they think I can speak to my pockets as a baker
to his loaves, and watch them rise in the sun?
Here, check my purse with your crow's-eyes,
it's empty, it's no more than an 80-year-old-fool
wheezing on bought women. Well I'm busy now,
I'm going to open my drowsy eyes lash by lash
and cannot be disturbed. Go knock at a door
that *has* a gold knocker, and secret *it* in your fist.

And if you whine at my window once more, I swear
the coins you seek so assiduously will be pounded
into your eyes for inspection, and weigh you down
as is the custom for corpses. The gold-dust you want,
it will collect on your shoulders as the common dust
coats figurines, and will afford you that much joy.
There are bars of silver to be impressed with your seal
when you topple from your servant-polished carriages
teeth-first. And you will not collect another ring
without its knuckle, grinding into your bulged cheeks!

The Exorcism Of Rule

Now I don't want to sound complaining again, but
there is a certain officer of the guard in this town
whose one wish is to see my neck dye the dirty napkin
lining his wicker basket. If I spit,
I've assaulted a priest. If I assault a priest,
Lord forbid my theorizing, I've sodomize-raped
a whole orphanage. Every time he sees me
it's the day for using the left nostril only
and there I am with my illegal right. Is it any wonder
I've been moved to making love with his wife?

So now I'm in the granary basement, shivering
among the sacks with my only friends for two days
the rats. We all have our cats to hide from.
I've paid my last coin, the good one
to pass any alchemist's test, to the old witch-woman
for a slogan that will work this time. So now
I charge you, fat-assed and basset-jowled
guardian of public safety, to leave my skin whole.
May your farts propel you across the embankments
to wreak your next vigil on eels and toads!

So now I'm spastic: my brow squints with the fervor
of a dog digging for fleas. You remember my eyesight,
my friends, that could pick out a crab
in a lady's bush across town —now I'm lucky
to spot the lady. Meat could roast
on my forehead. About the phlegm,
and the rheum, those nasty muds of the flesh,
the less said the better. And my body confuses
direction: my prick won't leap up, my food
won't stay down. Tell me, is it fair?

What I need is a wench with a body so fine
it will serve as a whetstone to hone the edge
of my vision on —that will keep me
looking clear! Yes, and she will fetch wine
home in a bottle cooled overnight
on the stream-bottom: balm
against fevered foreheads. What she will cook,
her exquisite nut-stuffed partridges, will
stay down; what leaps up —wow! Meanwhile,
my throat is sore as I sing this. Tell me, is it fair?

The Leave-Taking

Yes, we have come on hard times in this city.
Just yesterday I saw a cart of peas trundle by
—they were apples! The cart had three wheels on
and one chopped into a wooden leg for its driver.
There's a lady I know, she runs her business at night
and last week lost her pay when the expected cock
slipped into her was a knife —now she's sewn shut,
she's sharpened her teeth to be daggers. I want to go
someplace so peaceful, so plenteous —ah, but
if we write it in such times, it will never come true!

I'm going to the hills for a while, I hear
you can spear down game there with a toothpick,
and if you leave the door unlatched your only skulking in
will be the night air's, not a chill air, it curls
on your chest like a kitten. If you pluck a pear
from its branch another fills its place like drops
of water, no end to them, from a pipe-leak.
Rain drums stones, and all the air makes music.
And one can find women there who —ah, but
if I write what I know of, you'll crowd out there too!

Translation From Far Away

For some the cold, for some the heat. I've
two tins of tea remaining, enough
to fill this shed with a mallow cloud
and caulk even whisker-cracks
against the dry adhesion of ice, but mustn't
sip too soon after tramping in
from the zero season, for warm drink following
such gut-cold shatters teeth. They grow
more precious to an old man as they grow more
singular. So I rub mammalian temperature back
in easily, in levels, allowing the tongue to first
massage the gums, and almost I fancy I hear the crack
of spittle thawing. Then,
and only then, to my one spoon, the one they left me
with the yellowed bone handle, and into the sweet hill
of fern tea! There's a quiet, a pantomime-show, that occurs
at the kettle. On its metal-blue neck, such
thin separation of steam and chill, a tentative
moisture collects, and then the weightless edge of a slant
of the day's lilac lastlight collects
in *that,* implying progression, implying, specifically,
ascension, and such a one as is rendered by three purifying
stages of change. But
I bore you. I'm fine, as my hand —my organ
that's garrulous now— has already proved in this
rambling, and the exquisite cheeses
you sent arrived. When I break the wax rinds,
such a beautiful sour bouquet —!, the deer
have learned to nibble the milder, soapy curds
if mixed with pear bits. Exile,
my *chuchiks,* is not so bad. No.
The homeland, the past, from this distance takes on
a diorama's neatness and now
that it cannot be experienced can be
seen; and I have time for my philosophies,
and write, of course not for anyone
to read —the eyes of deer are much too

general for such discernment —but
if one believes there to be an order to things
one must place his things in order. A
maxim. Do not mind, the evening air accepts
my lectures. In winter, I adze the ice
for blubbery bottomfish, sometimes pecking the scales
clean before the throes cease; shadow
on frost communicates a nuance of color I lose
my concentration in, and some entire days are spent
in the valleys of violet and sloe-blue of liquid's
hardening. But, ah, in spring
the deer approach, a ragged phalanx
cleaving that first moist air, and the fronds unlock
their slow saps; I search
for lingonberry and furze. You must not
be sorry. I talk, when the Post arrives
once each third month, to the idiot
government courier, or when the Guard checks
on exile shed number twelve. They mumble
happenstance over mugs of my mountain cabbage broth,
and slice gray parings of caked dirt out
from behind their thumbnails onto the floor.
But best, I speak
to the deer, my crazy theories; their composure is their half
of the dialogue; I endeavor to learn
their speech. And in this way,
by daily accretion of numerous petty acts, the bucketing
dung, the alchemy of juices for ink, I fill
this warp-cracked square of shack with me
to its saturation, a bouillon, and do not miss
much of the days of brocade
and the parasol. The past's
excesses condense, as teawater to vapor, and thousands
of languid joys compress themselves in a single, intensified
studying how the ice melts. I think
the word to hack in timber
for commandment over a door like mine,
Accept. This winter
I've given the sense of touch
in my left leg, like a gift, to the landscape

and am not sorry for this reciprocative bringing
closer of the hills, only wonder
where my tactile sensation is, what form
it takes now, and to what ethereal use.
And some winter
soon —you must not wring your pastel initialed
lace hankies at this for I remember so well
the embroidered jonquils
and how they could not take abuse— I will set
out a greater package. Some winter, a fierce one,
even the eyes of the deer turn fogged, like
bad glass, their hooves take on the sheen of the purple
black, as in some coals, turns blacker with. Some cold,
some heat. And I will turn,
with its many dissonant creaks, my back
to the shack door and the heating kettle and journey
into the drifts with the enervating knee-to-waist
gait of the snow-walker, having expected it still
unexpectedly stepping beyond
where I have stepped before. And I will remove
the familiar cloth-patched fox gloves, staring
at vertical worlds, and watch my body leave
my body, in huge white breaths, as is the way
with winter, the lungs first
turned to that strange rigid steam, then
the chest and its blood-sodden
apparatus, the loins, and the legs, and the gristly rest,
and from the blue gullet the high thin whistle
the last tea announces escape with.

Making Old

In the old country there's a tin tub, almost
round, to bathe in with soap cut
straight from the cow. The milk
you can chew. The man you hate counts
every candle for the tax, even he gets
tea. Such tea.
The spoon floats on top. Ask
bubbie, ask *zaydie,* how wind
filled the pigs and everyone rode those
zeppelins to America from the scarecrow
with a turnip for a heart who closed
the old country, who closed down the old, the
old country.

    Shift.

A boy wakes. That is, his eyelids lift
but their dark side, like the moon's
in Verne or Heinlein, retains detailed
civilizations —this one,
bundled in a peddler's pack. Its wrist-thick
rope's undone. The townsfolk, hausfraus
mainly, gaggle around with their dozen roses:
ten raw knuckles rubied
on the washboard, and splotchy buttocks.
He gestures
grandiloquently through his buzzing cuff
of plumflies, and first hawks
the royalty items: eider-down gloves
for the sows' teats in winter, a cabbage-grate
with the Lord's Prayer. In the background, the bald ram
jacks its legs as a spatula pries
in, skimming the creamy rashes; the pus says
Kicking Disease. Two boys in the shape
of potato sacks chunk horse-chestnuts at the pond's
butcher-paper boat; its crew,
red ants, spread up the kerchief sail

like prickly-heat. There are songs
in the distance, indigenous tunes done in wheezing
ocarina music: Mary-Juggle-Two-Moons-And-Me-Lovebubs,
The Wee Whiskey Midwife, Our Whistling Flue. There are
gods in the ground as recently buried
as bruised forage, there are holydays: The Feast
of the Martyr's Larder, The Fast of the Ghost-Bees' Hive.
And, farther
than in the background, but no less causative
for abstraction, other forces
stretch their perennial sinews: primogeniture
drags its sodden muscle up the drainpipe; nipples,
like buds, clench
magnolias
of milk in from the frost; and
war, no more than a pear-hornet three counties over,
is shooting its waxy seed
in a crow that's not too high to be tracked
by the wolf, the slavering wolf, you want
for its fierce skin clipped to your shoulders. It's

my old country. Having none of my own,
I make it up, ersatz
root in my garden,
homeland without a home, and wait for the weather to age
the bones of the boys at the pond
to a validating brown, and the pond's gray taste
reach bedrock.

A Week On The Show

And he who has never felt momentarily what madness is
has but a mouthful of brains —Melville

40 on the stupid! —Sarah B.

CORRECT-O! And on to a new Step Up!
Gwendolyn Halverstrom, Newark housewife and mother of four,
for a new Gazelle-10 station wagon,
YOU are ready for your first Nifty Fifty! Good Luck and Here
    Goes:
What astronomical body circles the earth and has phases?

I believe it is the moon, Mr. Sphanks; and it has a cycle
as I recall of approximately thirty days.

CORRECT-O! And on to a new Step Up!
Gwendolyn Halverstrom, Newark housewife with pupils rich as
    inkwells, for a new Gazelle-10
YOU are ready for your next Nifty Fifty! Good Luck and Here
    Goes:
What astronomical body circles the earth and has phases?

From which the word *lunatic* is derived, Mr. Sphanks; they were
    chained
by the wrist to walls, or sometimes bolted to walls *through* the
    wrist,
as if the copper flavor of the blood should be bride to metal, and
    often
the head dunked in buckets of water was thought a cure and come
    winter
a few would be found with their faces frozen like rubble
in sheets of ice; then the family signed some papers.

CORRECT-O! And on to a new Step Up!
Gwendolyn Halverstrom, sitting up past midnight in Newark with
    candles
and garlic bouquets, for a shiny Gazelle-10
YOU are ready for your third Nifty Fifty! Good Luck and Here
    Goes:
What astronomical body circles the earth and has phases?

Green cheese, Mr. Sphanks; for the cheese she has holes and mould,
and lights on the hovel-floors in every nation, but green is reported
scarlet in the hold of the ball of cotton, and beaten gold
for a gong at the eardrum, and black in the land of the blind
where moon-sized holes edge out new skies from the retinal plate
and it hurts and the widow stares in the cotton's stink and wonders.

CORRECT-O! The Tooth is the Step of the Tongue!
Gwendolyn Halverstrom, dancing in Newark compacted
at the clitoral-tip like a match-head, for a new Gazelle
YOU are ready for your fourth Nifty Fifty! Luck bears our Ashes:
What astronomical body circles the earth and has phases?

And ebbs and swells, Mr. Sphanks; and wakes ahowl with grunion
at mine thighs, and the gates to the Salt-Mine in the blood
flung open for lock-shot and hinge-crack and then ken ye what but
    drown
from the inside out, Lady Sea being dominated a polyp
of kelp and coral too to the stars and housey-woman riding it,
    swimming not
so much in Source as depthing a brine-bottle in It the message
    reading
how this be the bottle the Sea she fits in, and then the beach, and
    bedsheet.

CORRECT-O! The Lung is the Foot on the Breath-Step!
   Gwendolyn
Halverstrom, clovequeen and fingerwhorls etched with spittle
turning Newark's alley-cobbles to deltas with life electrode in you
as in cue-chalk, skewering, skewering, NOW
for the slats are down and the scent of muff of Gazelle, as the hand
prongs five is the fifth of the gift and Luck the gland the Lord
   forgot:
What astronomical body circles the earth and has phases?

and how be the stars so close'n like moles on them udders
I sip she the lean white draught o' moonsheen down for all
   sex-come,
silky, silvery, in me throat, let bob, let bellow, Mr. Sphinx Of The
   Eye
Wink Wink Which Way Come British, and finish here me own
two dugs in rouge-n-taffywater and do with the shoes for kindling
   some and
run, then run, gone wax me flesh and vixen-once-with-wind-in-
   whiskers
and fish-nickel skin the next, wheesh, me, the hex-n-blessing, me
faces, me terrible Biochemical phases, Mr., schooner, ballooner,
   around
she Earth, come wing come hell-in-a-thimble, come blankety
   tuck-in Me
we fleeing stab-saddle back-o-My-Pretty me soot-city
root-tonic symphonical-in-a-dairy hair-like'n unto a cunt's-lawn
   gazelle

Narrative Continuity
—a poem in 10 chapters—

1.
I've always wanted to write a novel . . .

2.
"I have taken great pains
and gone to great expense to procure these
for your mistress, and now . . ." —and here
she extended one gloved hand in a gesture
of approbation withheld— "I fear
the culmination of all my arduous scrutiny
is demolished by this near-piratical action from a person
whose view of human nature is so emphatically base
as to allow him to initiate his heinous plans
with the nonchalance of a parlor-maid
dusting a figurine. I
am discredited!"

3.
. . . but have no knack
for narrative continuity, a Bedouin or thieving politician
always bouncing off the wrong mote
of Brownian motion, and a tangent
to my life becomes my life, as an amoeba's sticking
a trifle of itself out into the ecosphere
becomes the amoeba. I'm speaking
of locomotion in unicellular creatures
now, in the middle of what
was to be a love poem, see?

4.
And with those words
she turned upon her heel, leaving
the startled shopkeep to his surmisal of the universe
as a clockworks, and in the sunlit streets
was immediately abducted by a Bedouin
or a thieving politician.

5.
Meanwhile, back at the ranch,
a woman I love is leaving me. There is nothing
I can do or say to stop this, and a word
I use loosely, every day,
inevitable, is defined in the ridge
where the blouse is taut through anatomically-manifested
determination across the tightened bones of her
distant, diminishing back.

6.
I'm rethinking chapter 4 and revise the word *immediately*
to *welcomely.* In his desert tent he covers her
with kisses from head to foot, inbetween
the two of which he lingers, then slowly
undoes his robes and turban or
unzips his gray flannel pants and hangs them
so the crease keeps. Then his whole life enters
where he extends to her
like an amoeba.

7.
Or *I'm* leaving *her.* I always forget
which is which, my lack of narrative continuity always
confusing which side of the bed
initiates action, as if the Foil
pouting petulantly in one half of the blanket in
another world could be the Protagonist,
sympathized-with, wept-over —and this
befuddles the best friend
standing all day in the Brownian motion of dust rising
sunstruck off figurines
and ready to enter the plot with a bundle
of blame to lay
with a gloved hand imperturbably
on one of us or the other.

8.
Say it's the man
who leaves the woman,
Reginald. Even with a bloody
smack of loss and guilt
to either cheek, think, my
boy, of the freedom! That lack
in his life of continuity, of
knowing the next way-station
that the carriage pulls into is definitely
Falling-Actionshire, if you'll forgive
my trifling wit, is a way of saying anything
is possible! No, I guarantee you,
despite the onus of social responsibility,
this man we have imagined and tossed
so precariously about at our whims
to serve us, is let go
and serves no master now but
each new day, and who are we
to say that the next day's carriage is not
from an exotic land and laden
with adventure! Even now it's on its way,
and he may climb the howdah and ride off
whooping as gay as a Bedouin.
He's ecstatic!

9.
The chill sea slapped its face. The porpoises
had been fun, and the sea-horses
frolicked with it, zooming out
spawn from their bellies, each new wave cupped
new sun. But now
all was night, and was cold, and the giant
amoeboid creature had tossed it
hither and yon in a mucky polyp
with no regard for the straight line, and bitter
brackish water cut
deep in its hairline fractures. Oh
the world wasn't always easy for a porcelain figurine
come to life at the touch of a magic feather-duster! Swimming
home, to Dresden, across the Atlantic, from Tampa,
Florida, was no lark! And what
of the air force pilot, the rum-drunk Klondike dancehall girl,
her faithful collie, the one with the eye-patch
and ineluctable Georgian accent, weren't they
possible, weren't they due?

10.
Or he's sad.
In the final chapter
there is no resolution.
There is no climax.
A woman I love is leaving me.
There is no continuity.

A Journal Of The Plantations / *With Two Older Entries*
June, 1975

In the days of my sickness
I entered a wood, a half-light of vision
filtered through green and the simple, diminutive
sprigging of green vein, as if a correspondence
with my bloodworks. The night before had been no star
but cloud, and finally had released itself; now
each step pressed the storage of rain
out from loam, or moss, and even the light walk of chipmunk
weighed enough for the trampling
out of a thin, clear eke and its every hesitant claiming of ground
by paw left this vintage.

Know I have wasted this last Even spitted on a red branch of my
own Fever and turning continually in the flames thereof, so much
so that it seems a wonder my feather-mattress has not caught Afire
at the friction of my revolving. But the true Fright is not in this
constant turmoil of Agitations playing the Nerves or upheavings of
Rheum from the festers, so that every moment the Calm of the
Healthy Body is broken through Fever as is steady white Light
through a Prism, and thence to burn; no, but it is inside this Tu-
mult, a great sluggishness of the Blood is to be most feared, and
thrives there not unlike the Stomach-Worm that will imperturbably
feed no matter what the Flurry of a man's Body, will lie in its loops
and grow Heavy.

I stilled myself; and tried willing
even my heart to the composure of transport
in cellulose; and so it was, with every umber hair
on its body singular and attentive
as antenna, the chipmunk
approached. I could see its nostrils
scouring air, and the turn of forelimb muscle
tensing at each new inch's test, all the body
circuitry in caution. And, half a foot
from my boot, it halted in the uplifted primeval
pose of awareness, stood for a blink in its sensory
taking-in, then bolted —trusted
orange underbrush. *You'd better do better
than that, next time, little brother; no wonder
owls don't starve.* And, in correspondent
awareness of import —flinched, jerked
eyes up to what could have hovered
above me, felt for a blink the pinch-in of gray claws
of nerve, from my own unimpassioned, around
my own vulnerability.

*Assayed the Forest, walking with care lest I tire myself overly. But
no pace is so slow, no not even a limp, but it misses Immeasurable
Detail overflowing any Spore, or Mite, for Nature is Lavish in such-
wise that any common garden Snail bears, to the patient eye, a
Cornucopia on its back, and the climate, and Commotion, of a
single leaf that can be fit in the Palm shames our grandest Metrop-
olis. A Finch sewed the pasture. A Lichen made the hall-table
Paisley to be dull. But the next Amazement, attendant upon the
initial, is how, in all this seeming Otherworld Abundance, a man
snaps comfortably in Place —the Mites could nest his ear, would
he Will it. And under his newfound Wonderment at the leaf in his
Palm, as under the leaf, is his Wonderment at the Palm itself, that
the leaf not even as thick as some Paper has given such Depth to
his Hand, and shown such a green Door to pass and be home
through.*

. . . No owl. Nothing
more foreboding than sky admitted by shuttling
of leaves, sky sized to winking
leaf-shape —oblivious, blue
stares. And crossing the plank bridge, as
the poem took shape, it built itself
in instinct
around two yellowed diary extracts, perhaps an overturning of
where its roots held; support. On the stream
a water-spider maneuvered
six miniscule cushions of air, and this
I took to be a star
of david, a sign; that,
though our steps are numbered, for a time
there is balance   /as in the perfect coating
of the eye/   between
the immiscible rightness of body
and the intervening of sky.

For The Day

Dear Alan: I dreamt we were impressed.
We sat in a room, maybe two of fifty
guys focusing on a TV set
as if to teleport it, when a rifle butt cracked
the door down, soldiers poured in almost
as if from a hydrant, in full bayonet
regalia, and to a man we were shanghaied
into the Lithuanian Army. This is
the truth. Some parts are fuzzy but others
gleam with portraits of you and me
against a tintype background, and it's this
lapse and clarity in alternation I think
convinces me the dream could be honest
biography; a full account I'd mistrust.
The time: indeterminate: an 1890 capital
or 1975 hamlet; lots of wood, buildings
shingled and citizens straight as planks
though some still apple-cheeked rather
like two-by-fours not yet given up
blooming; pushcarts, derbies, and there
we were, privates on patrol. I guess we passed
basic training, and none the worse.
Our uniforms were dun, but the buttons shone
like small suns against a dusty plain,
and made enough show. We were confident
and swaggered, and reached the high apples
for the little girls, proffering them with a polish
of our starched cuffs, and winking assurance
to the greengrocer; all the while we bantered
urbane witticisms and never doubted
we'd soon escape through the quarry forest
maybe dressed as charwomen or smudged dung-boys
out to pail a good day's fuel; and this
lark, this small vacation, this comedy
of errors simply spiced our usual repartee.
We were strolling the promenade with a Hans
or Lars —I can't quite remember— a smiling
ox-shouldered lout we must have met

in goose-step class, and trading
our metropolitan buffoonery among the shops,
when Hans or Lars leaned on the door
with a sign in Lithuanian reading DON'T
LEAN ON THE DOOR; it was brutal.
Who knew? or knew to know; but a sergeant
bloodied Hans's face with a huge meat-cleaving fist
out of nowhere, and he emptied like a sack
on the ground; it made a vein of the gutter.
This is the truth. And I'm not proud:
but we kept walking on, as if our backs
could lid our eyes to the scene; we had our plans
you see, important plans; we had a place to get
home to. And we said by the silence
between us that we knew now we were watched,
and just two buttons on a starched Lithuanian
uniform so huge it basketed the nation
in its stiff sleeves; and we couldn't sweat
if the rule-book said it was cool outside,
or ever impersonate officers for a frolic,
ever again; or grimace, or limp, or carol.
But though I'm not sure what happened
over the next few years, only that we were good
soldiers —and scenes of lavishing bear-fat
on boot-toes for hours on end come to mind—
I do know we never gave up the hope
of escape; I don't see us planning escape,
and perhaps we didn't —we never forgot
Hans or Lars— but a feeling permeates
this dim-lit decade, much like an itch
while sleeping: not bad enough to wake you
but, under the monsters and rose-tit courtesans,
there. Maybe it's all that kept us going.
Or maybe we did scheme while peeling potatoes
and add one line a day to a plan passed
secretly in a hollowed spud; I don't know;
but, whether any lieutenant recognized it,
a subtle nuance of North Side Chicago
clanged like frosted trash can lids
through our Yessir, No sir in Lithuanian.

There were good days, and bad days;
equal, I guess. Exercise was no joy,
or war games. But I see us sometimes lounging
at an outdoor cafe, a carafe of white wine
on a cream-and-red-checked tablecloth,
slicing cheese beneath a wicker awning
and bartering garrison gossip for news
of town goings-on with the waiter. Saturdays
were our days off, and we saw two plump
town shopgirls; surely they minded their dress,
bobbing like cork above whatever neckline
was in fashion; yet I see them always in bright
peasant garb, with scooped necks smiling
under a fleshy expanse of breast, and heavy drape
dresses a lightweight man
could hammock in; they were always laughing,
and we were always telling jokes. Eventually,
one Saturday, we married, the wine more white
than ever, the cheese more sweet —a dessert cheese.
They were good to us, and one Sunday when we woke
up middle-aged we hardly noticed; and all
distinguishing us from any two parasol'ed couples
snoozing Sunday in an arbor shaded
from the great Lithuanian sun was the eye
I'd open, or you'd open, much like a knot
in a paneled wall through which can be seen,
for a second, the forest
it grew in and put forth fruit from.
And then we'd wink shut.
The lopped-off limb still itches; that's medical
fact; and this is the truth. And then of course
I woke from my dream,
and scratched myself wide-eyed,
Alan, alone in my bed,
and buttoned up for the day.

The Miles

Fair? You expect a *corporation* to be *fair?*

                                        —a trade house editor

Dear Liz: A dream. For which I offer
no exegesis. What lapses and obscurities
cloud it, like old glass —like old glass,
authenticate; and, in fact, it begins
in swampmist. A woman, in white
film, with silver hair thick
as kelp, broke from fog; she had wrists
as clear as a blue run of trout
underwater, she had no name, she saw
primally —that is, not an infant's
first light through the wash of silver nitrate,
or even the operated's sudden release
from glaucoma —but: a seeing as if the first
of a genus, how optics never spangled
before in genetics of quite this
chandelier cut. She was gentle, and protected
on either side by a creature of fantastic
aspect —black, low, cockroach
carapace —think your ear to an ebony
vinyl pillow picks up the cluck
of a spider's heart. And these two
paleozoic vestiges, like a nervous system's
mine detectors, scoured the ground
at her feet. I can only say
she was worth more than any one
human life —a sudden knowledge like the fruit
seen when dyes expose the tree
in the brain— then the narrative
bubbles —old glass— and clarifies into a scene
of confrontation: the first woman,
halted, appalled, stares facing
a second: whose portrait remains
vague, though flashes of diamondback
snakeskin armor play in my mind like wattage
on anthracite —that, and hair like spool

upon spool of the wire that knifed across
eastern Europe, the kind where rust seemed blood
the air let in passage. Liz,
she was evil. —And flanked by two leashed wolfhounds
snapping jaws as if a mouse should scent the feetsmell
of cheese at their throats' backs. This woman
laughed. The plot
warped, and —such
autonomous gerrymandering of storyline convinces
me of something in this vision approaching the formidable
veracity of objects— there was a mansion, of many
blade-edged defensive outjuttings, as if
chitinous. Here, an old Scotsman in a plaid
wheelchair came to call —he was the lucid woman's
paladin: sixty years old, quick-tempered
face like an eruption of righteous indignation across
which a moustache flexed gray wings and
hovered. Three things: his eyes were kind; his arms,
from the wheeling, were terraced; his tongue
revolved in his brogue
like a gerbil. But he wasn't
speaking now, but the other man, the lord
of the mansion, the wolf-woman's blood-initiated
vizier-of-sorts, and every word
was gatling, and in the palm of one hand: pale,
reed-thick, the lucid woman's
hair —see wounded
floss. What happened, why
the paleozoic sentinels failed, is lost
in an unrecorded REM —suffice
to say here was the booty, how the vizier said
he had 90% of her hair now and the law
supported his claim to the other 10%, he was of
fierce mien. The law of strong
take all. And that's why the epigraph, intrusive
though it is, at this letter's top: perhaps the dream,
like La Brea, at one point surfaced
into conscious light. But in the dark
settling of that mansion the vizier, his jugulars
working like oars, clenched the pillaged hair

in a chainmailed fist and threatened the full force
of his minions. "We
desire that hair, and shall have that hair,
old man. The amassing of power
at our disposal is beyond your ken, the
rat hordes that have tunneled the blue
sperm whale in minutes, the red ants dancing
like small print in litigation, do not
oppose us charlie. My veins, like laboratory
tubing, circle the same spat of acid that drove
such forebears as Patricide Flann, the man who rolled
on lampreys for condoms, a woman whose tongue served
for the ladle in a tureen of bubonic plague, Mad
Sam whose victims were packed into so many
thousands of thimbles, and, worse, the
saner ones: whose money owns the eye
at your keyhole, the cop's finger pointing like polaroid
at your most intimate moments, the name
on your check, the world's
ore, the man with a lever connected directly
to your hunger pang, oh don't
fuck with us buddy." His chin
made a fist. And the Scotsman
looked up from a sore
brooding nod, and only said, slow,
in a most level tone, "Have ye hearrrd
of the good ship *Molly Malloy*, that they said
of herrr *ye rrreach old Molly and prrray
to see home?* Have ye hearrrd of that ship, lad?
I'm THAT Captain Jack." And the vizier's
mouth dropped like a moth to the floor, in
throes there, and his eyes broke like plates. And
in that moment I knew, Liz, how
it would turn out okay for people
like us. And then there was a wet hill,
in the sunlight, and wheelchair tracks
leading up to the summit, like rails
along which a great locomotive of air ate
up the hard miles.

1.
Jogging / Dear W.Z.:

Goyishe doilies —Wayne, my mother
was right; you're *different*, an intricate Christmas
flake, one lace snow,
on each plump couch-arm. There are these

spaces between us. Your duck-blood soup.
Your wall so crossed it's
arlington. Your wife, her supple cat
fur in the darkness / my
onan-women. Though you WASP-stinger
surgeried it to a truncated Zade, you
brother to bowling ball, you
grandson to sausage,

Zajdzinski. Now that we've both escaped
Chicago's concrete Aviary for Comatose Pigeons,
you west / me east, now their gray peck
for crumbs doesn't show in our eye-twitch,
I dream

fancifully of your old apartment on Hamlin
and a doily
as the white nerve-webbing
a battered bird of paradise hinges
its two wild wingsweeps together
with. I guess I mean my mother's ethnic drawing
away as correlative of physical distance; but
the lace system, sensory
filigree, plied through

that bird —connective tissue. Remember
braving the midtown bus to *Deep Throat?* The story
behind every thumbprint oiled onto a new stop's fare
was voyeurism. This is what
men share. And other stories,

your grandfather bludgeoning the dreamless
foreheads of beefcows —the stockyard's
jeweler, the carats of blood. You shared his apron
with me, red map in your closet. Once,

in a letter, you spoke of our jobs: ". . . they'll
use us. No more, no less." And then "I
send you warmth. Write back." Missouri's
stunted trees have provided
knots, hard focal points, for your writingpaper.
And I'm hoping some of my words will prove tinder

for upstate New York's forsythia
blaze. I write I'm jogging
lately, the try for even, serial
breaths to relax me. You
listen. Sometimes, our letters, passing
each other in transit: a cross
of the fingers. For luck. The longer the distance,
the stronger, maybe. We'll see. Now

remember, Lovelace, the idea of Lovelace
going down on a full house
in darkness . . .

The reason, flush in Chicago's rush-hour
bus, we sense the impersonal
sexuality of stranger on stranger

is: linen —the cheap weave
of strand next to strand, the crowding
in of bodies. I was crushed to the workings
under an orange skirt, it almost
burnt me, and then she shimmied
off at her corner. Her night . . .

the common bedsheet, though it has its
tight, muslin, immediacy
—it's the paced breaths inbetween
that make lace exquisite.

And so I think of you.

2.

Clotting / Dear Ginnie:

Outside of Groton, surrounded by nothing
but clover popcorning the acres, and holding
a rickety sentinel's stance above its claim to
pasture grazed by little
more than earthworm and buck hare
—a house's framework, savaged by fire,
takes the wind for its password. Five,
maybe six, miles up toward Freeville, goldenrod
burns the eye like Mathew Brady's snapping
Atlanta; and, nearer still, a hand's count of milch-cows
circles cud. Their rubbery lips herd
stream in. A calf looks buckled to one, teat
almost a prong for attachment, the whole a plush
doll set, in quietude and relation. But

here, two-storied, this once
house, only scorched outline now
and debris, frames what kindling
bits weren't worth the salvage, against
that green-blue background; Freeville's
faroff elm-tasseled sky —this
house, implicit study
of light dividing natural boundary
from wreckage. Broke pipes, cracked
blackened lintel dangle like the testimony
of singed strands fringing a powderburn
in the fabric of a tapestry

of family life. I remember the scene, stitched
in nascent rain and the billowy gray plumes
of mismanaged charcoal: your father
in his boxer shorts knighting elf-high invisible
supplicants with his well-suckled magnum of mash,
your mother picking stuck flies off the butter. And
the homilies worked with the best of intentions in
raw silk below: *Blood is thicker than water.*
Home is where the heart is. Once, in conversation, I
punned: *hurt.* You laughed. But your letters, now
that you've torn the last thread that moored you
to backwater Fox Grove, Illinois, show little
respite: "This world isn't worth your destroying
yourself . . . I got my manuscript together: *Look,*
You Need Trouble." Your writing hurts. And my writing
to you tonight is, first, to quote a 19th-century journal
I've been helping update: "Blood is thicker than water
because of fibrinogen, which heals
all wounds. Fibrinogen
tries like a logjam." And I dream wood,
the skeletal
late-19th-century planking in
ruin in Groton, this X-ray of what remains from attempt
at interlocking —the wood
wants to knit, wants the underground
rootweave of clover. So, second, I want to quote the dream

itself: a long, dark house
at night, a shape self-contained
and stable. Just that: a light-black that's the solitude
of sky, and a heavy black oblong of solace. And
one lit square in the upper-right corner that's
your room, or my room, perhaps suggesting a profile
bent in communication. It's typing
Warmth, Albert. It's sending Best, Gin. This corner window
I saw was meant as the postage stamp
—a face, relaxed, in lampglow. And I knew that one wakeful
consciousness moving the slow house through
to morning was the presentiment of the
old wood fleshing new blueprints —the wish in this
letter to you.

3.
The Reunion Sonnets / June 1975

                    for Michael
                    (and in memory, R.S.)

In this photo we're in Mexico City, in suits.
It's 1964. Our ties are as thin as the paper they're
developed on. In one year Von Steuben
High School will slap our rumps
into the world and in ten years it will be
today. The Class Reunion. We have to wear
suits. Or they won't welcome us into restaurants
and will think all Americans boors. Don't say
Americans. They're Americans too. I'm so skinny
in this picture I'm draft-exempt. At the Reunion
they'll ooh, they'll how-skinny-you-were. Alan's
tie is so skinny. A vein. Now they'd just hitch
with one pair of jeans and a knapsack. My students.
Ten years. We're smiling. We're Kennedy fans.

We watch Twilight Zone. Rod Serling's cool
and creepy every week, but now it's summer so we're
in Mexico City. Then. Three smiles: 1. ∪ 2. ∪ 3. ∪
It's summer vacation. Ellen says don't scratch
the bug-bites, just make little red hot-cross buns
of them with my thumbnail. Okay. You don't know her,
now, ten years. She thinks I should lose weight. My ties
are fat. We eat enough for an army then suffer
turista after those pink things. They'll serve green
hors d'oeuvres and say oh so this is Ellen we've heard
about you. It's creepy. On a Twilight Zone once a man
took photos of the future. He could look into the future.
We're smiling. I'm smiling up at myself. I'm looking
hard in the camera. Who could guess fat ties?

Did you guess about Kennedy? There's a bullfight. The word
assassin. We'd read it. We wouldn't say it, ever, for four
months. Once a man knew Lincoln would get it but no one
believed him. That's a good one. They rerun them, now.
In the summer. The bites are bad. Ellen knows what to do
but she's eight. Alan's seventeen. He's a smile on top
of a thin tie, a graphic crutch. And don't drink the water. Tell
them about the taxi driver who asked if we wanted
muchachas. That's a funny one ten years later. Then I'd date
Phyllis. Then we dated. Now they just seem to bump and enter
and part in a daze. My students. It bothers me,
ten years. Ellen says not to scratch. If it hurt
there were crutches. But it didn't hurt, we're smiling.
In the background are men without legs who want our money.

Our parents' money. The Class Reunion can fuck itself. A bundle
of bread just to see how fat Nancy Tannenbaum's got? Uh-uh. Or
    whatever
her name is now. She was sweet. I'm not going. I went,
I took pictures, at Xochimilco my tie caught sun like tinder and
the water stank, that's enough. I write you and sometimes we meet
in New York. I met Ellen in a class of mine. My students. They do
dope across the border, like I did homework. Ten years. You look
the same really. I guess your hair's longer. I haven't worn a suit
since . . . Look, do you remember the one where they go back
in time? Alan's saying: What for? —The muchaches. We fucked
ourselves a lot then. Not much else. I'm glad we write. I'm glad
we share something. Veins in the same time. Same
station. Tonight Rod Serling died. I'm crossing my bites. We're
here, Michael, and we're tied.

From The Physical To
treatise & dream

And when he rose from four legs to two, above the bestial sniff-at-the-asshole, what did Man lose? Ernst Haeckel postulates that olfactory sensation was the original sex attractant, in the primeval water, and linked the first two cells. In the black, in the back caviar of the body, the farflung progeny of one of those cells still lathers in each of us. What we gained, of course, was a richer brain: the ability to conceptualize, to remove the rose from the nostril and say "the rose is *like*. . . ." "the rose is *named*. . . ." "the rose can be made better. . . ." A step, in that leap to two feet: from the physical to the functioning-beyond-physical; or —a little closer to being a ghost.

*

As if I mattered to anyone today. I gave directions, pointing confusedly with my ink-whorled fingers to someone in a tweed cap; I made the Office Chatter, and they made the Office Chatter with me, and we were witty, and walked out separate doors to the char-gray rain, and what the day had to offer has washed off a yellow raincoat, and only a pale remembrance of ink still clings in my thumb's congenital relief map, and even that's going fast. . . . We *are* ghosts. For the difference I made, or they made, we passed *through* each other, not even giving the little that remains to inform an X-ray. It might only be weeks —or days— till I fumble my nicked keys at the office door, stumble through and plop in the chair's three creaks, and hear them wonder what eerie wind has entered the building and rustled the shuffle of papers on Goldbarth's desk. . . .

There are ghosts, and there will be more ghosts, they exist in the past or in extrapolation, there is the ghost of my arm, in my arm, as I write this, it wants to rise like chalk-dust from the trough, there are ghosts, they long to settle. A handsome Italian lover is hovering over the lotioned dildo, he is mist, he is hardening muscle, he is fog, the ghost of sexual loneliness clasped in its plastic case. A plowman, a ruddy-faced lout in his 40's, is plying the left breast of the wet-nurse, he has fathered every child she's given suck to for fifteen years, she wears him between her two great rubbery tits like a pendant, he's real, he's fading, he's a sepia neuron, he strokes her to sleep, there are ghosts. *You dinna hear o animals wi' ghosts.* Or of animals with anguish.

❋

I'm talking, I guess, about politics —that is, national priorities. And what's most important, here in this one squat Greyhound Bus Station serving as a link in the country's nervous system, is movement. The bus has democratized twentieth-century rapidity, call it *mobility* it's a good thing, call it *goodbye* and the straw-hatted geezer with liver-spots weighing down his hands is in the corner near the yellowed tub of drinking water, trying hard not to cry. There are hands here, and hands at airports, and hands at the docks, and at taxi stands, waving *farewell* so fast, they disappear. You can prove it, cut and shuffle a deck of birth certificates . . . see? Or: there's an alley cur with its leg lifted, pissing declamatory stink against the Greyhound Station wall. And there's a line of a hundred thumbs on the highway, hitching; the sun goes clear through them some days.

Hey: it's a dream we all have —the most sober of us wakes with it shaking him once a year: that we fling the door open —it's storming outside, huge thunderheads like worried brains in the sky— and enter the office on all fours, howling, upsetting the grapefruit rinds from the wastepaper baskets . . . There *is* something in that ring of dogs this morning, circling snout-to-ass like a backyard Uroborous, endless and whole. There's a tiny pink rose beneath the she-dog's tail. The petals open. Close.

Mammalogues

1. *Dolphin:*   Monologue & Song

Once I approached you. What you call
a hand was perforating
water. Then you reached land
and walked. But the hand knew.

> *Now I will sing you the dolphin song:*
> *The sperm is a fish.*
> *The fish is a lung.*

Sometimes, my eyes go opaque
as scale. And then the clarifying rush
in of air shocks, and
quickens. I could envy you this.

> *A fish out of water is dead*
> *Or is Man. The blood's where it ends.*
> *The sea's where it began.*

And I understand it as the link.
The distinction between sea and blood
is a subtle chemistry neither you nor I know
with the finesse of shark.

> *The ocean's inside, and heart*
> *Moves its tides. Under the moon*
> *Men swim into their brides.*

So we're both warm. Sometimes
you give a touch that's warm,
one in a series. I'm
a touch. That could be the division.

Inside a woman the coming-home calls.
The cunt is a gill.
The cock hears and swells.

It's this: I tried it. Once, I tried
a thumb, that theory of opposition.
But then I decided to build my city with
no tool but a spine.

> *The ear is a shell.*
> *To make love makes oars.*
> *Head next to head, the birth-water roars.*

And I live here. We
live here, and signal, and rub
up love, and reason,
in tactility. Look . . .

> *Some are born single,*
> *Some tied close by skin.*
> *But always, in brine, everyone has a twin.*

If the gray of the brain, in its motherblood,
could fashion its body as like itself
as possible . . . Look, we
do envy the "wheel." But I'm saying . . .

> *He knows you. He knows that you dream*
> *Of the splash. You know him by breathing.*
> *The lung is a fish.*

You say what could be done
without hands? We say this
is what hand could do
freed from the body.

2. *Ursus:* Speech & Text

On the cave wall, the bear, rendered small
by a brushstroke, says: I who am ten feet tall
   at the shoulder, all claw, all appetite,
am with you, through the Neanderthal night
   now, in comforting size, and can be carried
compactly as the future in a gene. Carved, buried,
   I will be your fat, and your skin, protectively
all winter, and you will remember me.   /So

   sleep. There will be many transformations and pacts
between us, but now the only facts
   you need know are a child's text:
yes, people die; yes, there may be a next
   world and a waking. Light will fill the den,
and clarify its totemic zoo, and the eyes will open
   and hands hug something familiar, the renew-
ing orientation. It's Pooh. Pooh says: I remember you.

Clock Invention

1.
The Earl of Sandwich is standing around
in the 18th century, wondering
what to do with two slices of chewy bran-studded bread
and a torso of roast beef. Could he
make some kind of sachet out of this? Would it look
regal, stitched with gold hawks and hung in the pantry?
The 18th century stinks, like oil
trapping rainbows on the soup, drift colorfully
around his talcum-dusted wig, which is filled
with many conundrums, of which this is merely
the latest. When *you* appear
in that sudden magnesium burst we associate so strongly
with flashback in fiction, and whisper
solemnly at the pool of lilac-water in his ear "shave
the meat between two slices of bread, how
convenient, how strange they never thought of it decades before,
like pantyhose, now you can go check the kennel-hounds
and lunch simultaneously, you will be famous John Montagu
4th Earl of Sandwich, your name
on the tip of everyone's tongue." You can see, then, of course,
the many problems inherent in time travel.

2.

Casket-sturdy
grandfather clocks in their soldierly veneers,
Bavarian cuckoos with ox-healthy peasant maidens parading
their cowcatcher wooden busts out the door, water
clocks with their chronal bungholes . . . There are plans
for the construction of
what for lack of a more appropriate phrase must be termed
a musical instrument —consisting
solely of timepieces, all varieties, finicky
stopwatches, eggtimers counting three minutes
of Death Valley, watches in pendants so two hands
will always point at milady's billowy breasts, pocket
watches, pacemakers like blacksmiths in hearts . . . And composers
will set these, each to its own time, whatever
the symphony calls for, I don't mean the music
of ticking and chimes, no
sensationalism —I mean the subtle orchestration of 6:15
in a roseate Australian dawn, with the cosmic prick
of time when Muhammad was born from a steamy burst
of waters into the chill desert air —I mean the tension
and difficult liaison between noon in the Alps,
with all its connotations of mid-day or ale
in capped pewter tankards, and just the squeeze
of breath in the moment before an otter displaced his own
sunned volume of coral-diddled ocean and
Lee Oswald hit the trigger. . . . Isn't
this the art we wanted all along, this cathartic
implying of knowledge. . . . Though in the long run we expect
it will enhance, and not assuage,
most questions.

3.

That is to say, who
invented the sandwich? Not the Earl, if you popped
back from 1975 and planted that fertile idea, miniscule
and redolent as oregano, in his head. But
not you, for weren't you born in a world
in which the sandwich was a given, as accepted
as all the eternal verities —taxes, the rise and fall
of the hem? At that radiant moment when roast beef
hummed minutely, like a radio, in affinity
for *ménage à trois* with the bread, did you *both*
invent the sandwich? Or, as in Buddha's queer parables,
did neither?
It would be like our love,
dear —now
tempestuous as magenta roses shrilling from tight dark buds
with the resplendence of alarm clocks, now thinning
between us like taffy— for which
neither you nor I is willing, credit or blame,
whirlpool or cornucopia,
to take responsibility.

4.
I have a clock,
a piñata, and it strikes the hours
in minutes of candied gnat's-eggs, jellied mayfly-bodies,
sugar-powdered pistils and stamens fencing
in time-lapse photography. I have a clock,
a magnifying-lens, with its one hand telling the hours
in sun, with its seconds and parsecs stampeding like ants,
the human pupil spreads in it like a bead of black oil
in bathwater. Pinheads used to be clocks, a way of saying
Time's ubiquity, for they were the smallest things but held Time
fully, as well as could, say, alluvial plains
or ocean bottoms; now
the angels howevermany skate on the iridescent rinks
of neutrons, spirochetes, amino acids, and score
eternity there with their silver blades; and all the anachronistic
pinheads collect in my velvety pincushion heart
like discarded chimes. But I have a clock,
a small intestine with the minutes marked off
in villi, it means a timepiece need not be round, we suffer
horizontal passages of chronology, a human life
is one, and some things, say like the thinklines trenched
in your mind with the individuality of fingerwhorls, unlike
History, will not repeat. And I have a clock,
a lover, the days pass in shapes cut out against the gray horizon
like adrenalin waves; a clock,
the moon being eaten; a clock, the panties going round
from noon to midnight in the washing machine; a clock,
the blood on their crotchpiece. I have
a tangerine in the fridge, a speck of lamplight hitting
my Kennedy for President button, the buzz that lives
in the phone, a pen, a bottle of after-shave
shaped like Buddha and every morning he's clearer, a window.
I have a clock.
Plankton.

5.
Nobody's ever slapped salami's mauve rump
with a whitewash of mayonnaise, and bedded it down
between rye slices thinking: I've made one great hell of a
goldbarth. There are problems,
and there will continue to be problems, so long
as spacemen gone two years to Neptune return
as their great-great-great-great-grandchildren; even now
the light in which we met
and made a winch of our tongues cranking up
endless buckets of bodily juice:

is being developed
on film for the delectation of whatever taste may function
as voyeurism in a carbon-based biology, is
growing sharp, and clear, in interstellar darkrooms for the first time
—although here on Earth, when I mention it, or
you, depending on who's most angry, it
fades suddenly from our minds. There are problems,
there is a clock whose cogs are jewels
still unmined, still turning in the turning planet.

6.
Come, let us go
watch the hounds frisk among the pliant rosebushes,
pink sweets of saltwater taffy sucked by all
of your glistening sets of lips. We will set up
a side of roast beef, with a kitchen-knife in
like Excalibur, on a pedestal.
For our sundial. For the blade's shadow,
for the light on the meat.

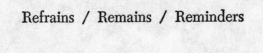

Refrains / Remains / Reminders

1.

Off Etna Road, a house
burned cellar-flush still reeks
weeks later with exposure of the ancient pulses
that ripple tree-rings
through wood. Starlings land on slats, peck
routinely, then flap
up a scatter of ash, bearing
hamlike smokestink in their belly-feathers
for miles, gray haze
in gray avian shapes growing faint in the far gray sky
swagged over Ithaca, New York. For I've come east
from where the backditch barns in Utah
shine like sugar cubes, for I've seen lumber
gain three-hundred years, horizontal
archaeology, digging telltale mounds replaced
by doing Route 80, and now,
near the nation's first edge, a board
burnt out of its framework gives
three centuries of solidity up
to air. Its system is bare, and sun
assumes the volume of farmhouse
in what's left, the bent piping, the
bowel of the place, the black sac
veined in rootworks. And
these saplings, even, scaled
stegosaurian with char, take on
the implication of all prehistoric remains,
until the light goes thick
with lush ghost-forests from
long before logs
—deciduous, huge, original
handles
the national scroll unrolled from. For I
have come east, never having been east
before: I've come back, come
home, to sing the song of the smouldering posts
10 miles out of Ithaca, New York.
It's gray. The few fall leaves
the frost missed
torch the skyline.

2.

The mind too has a cellar. A boy,
16, squats in the underground stores of Furstenberg's finest
whiskey-mill, grinding
potato in the swampy dark —when
Niederhoffer's drunk,
foreign recitation, incomprehensible but
for its musics, entices the boy
upstairs, and certain schnapps-blurred words
TELEMACHOS, PERSEUS, ARGOS, blank out
the morning of herring, brooms, bags of salt, they
light, with a single heady beam, the mental
coalbin where for ten years his father's stories
of heroes and quests have been a coma in him —now
they stretch, they lift shields. Nobody,
while the bulls tip
into cows' accommodation, while the kettles announce
hot lunch-water through the syncopated town,
while the clouds mass, nobody
thinks it a day in the green leeks of Furstenberg
different from any other, but "I
wept bitter tears over my own unhappy, uneducated
fate. Three times over did I get him to repeat
those divine verses, rewarding his trouble
by three tots of schnapps, which I bought
with my week's only pfennig. From that moment on
I never ceased to pray God that by His grace I
might yet acquire the happiness
of learning Greek." The clouds break. It's 1838, just 35 years before
❄

Ebbinghaus will begin his famous
memorization of TAJ, ZIN, VEC, YOX, DAC,
attempting to formulate how many nonsense-units
the trained mind can hold, for how long; and Jung
will postulate a hominid fossil
buried, countless millennia deep, in the bottom-most stratum
of braincell.

3.

Sometimes, on some nights,
a photo, or, more accurately, the memory
of a photo, shapes
in the gray meats of thought, and I see
through varying thicknesses of mist
a boy
in a hooded playsuit arcing
the long fling of stick
for a sofa-sized alleydog he loved
enough to think he'd find trace
of retriever. Well,
sometimes; if no fresh bitch's-turd
or dropped popsicle confused him,
Duke could fetch. There would be
songs about squirrels in teakettles
to hum, or string to wind
and unwind, while waiting. Later, the stick,
like a memory, would come back,
flecked with dog-slop and teeth-marked. The dog
would die, or at least undergo the physical space of a being
given away that meant death, and the boy
would pucker his eyes like cut flesh
against this. There would be
books he'd keep place in
with one torn nerve draped over the page, and
questions, there would be sets of curtains
for clocks in his life, and his hand's first
milking of semen. The dog
would come back, sometimes sharp, sometimes
gray, as if leaping from a gray
photographic bath. Or, sometimes, just
the photo itself, with the arm raised and maybe
that stickend caught in the process
of knocking against the air,
frantically, all night,
as if asking
admission
into the present tense.

The talking dog
Richard Wilbur quotes in February, 1969,
in his lecture Poetry And Happiness,

> Brick—old yellow bricks, crumbling with age in a garden-
> wall; the sweet breath of young cows standing in a moun-
> tain-stream; the lead roof of a dove-cote—or perhaps a
> granary—with the mid-day sun on it; black kid gloves lying
> in a bureau-drawer of walnut-wood; a dusty road with a
> horses' drinking-trough beneath the sycamores; little mush-
> rooms bursting through the rotting leaves . . .

It's Doctor Dolittle's
Jip, his nose
compartmentalizing air. Wilbur says,

> A catalogue of that sort pleases us . . . it stimulates that dim
> and nostalgic thing the olfactory memory, and provokes us
> to recall the ghosts of various stinks and fragrances.

The concept of poet
as maker of lists.
And a man could carry
a page like that in his shirt pocket
all his life for its devoted, dog's
retrieving
of the past, could watch it,
like all old paper, brown
and harden with age, as if
in attempt
to bring back something of the feel
of the original tree.

✢

"The charting of the comparative depths of Shakespearean sonnets
and water currents
has never been finished, and which —those fissures
sectioning the brain, or
those carving central New York with its creek system— holds more
is problematical. Thought
and carnality
ever collide, cross, and separate, like two courting hawks
on a graph." The lecturer
asks that the lights be dimmed, and flashes
his audience the magnification,
wall-sized, of a boy
on gray park grass, with his gray Duke, and great
gray stakings-out of happiness.

4.

He learns English: 6 weeks. Spanish: 6 weeks, French,
Dutch, Portuguese, Russian, Swedish, Polish,
Italian: 6 weeks each. Always, the past, filtered into
and through him, takes shape in the future, beckoning
on, and captions from scenes lit
by torch-pitch in the epics burst in his own life like flares:
ATHENA VISITS TELEMACHOS. THE SAILORS
CHANGED TO SWINE. Spitting brine,
blood, and teeth, the shipwrecked 19-year-old
cabin boy grips beach as if to fuck it:
1841. CHARYBDIS VOMITS THE SEA
INTO TURMOIL. Business: a brother's gold rush
estate quintuples in Cuban sugar,
South American hemp, guns run
toward the Crimean War, blue jewels of sweat
in United States cotton, now there are business
travels: rickshaw, sampan, howdah, St. Petersburg
thighs waxed with sex-mucuses of court ladies. THE
SIRENS MESMERIZE. He divorces
Ekaterina, discovers Sophia, "my dear wife,
an Athenian lady, who is an enthusiastic admirer
of the classics, and knows almost the whole of the Iliad
by heart," there are people, they touch
and crumble in touch, they are suites
in each other like Great Themes in literature, they
break tokens, they leave, they return. THE OLD DOG
ARGOS WAGS TO SEE HIS MASTER BACK. There
are dreams, there are long horizontal
patterns we think of as lives, there are tapestries: nightingales
rising from trees, there are threads
for the wings, threads to root with. ODYSSEUS
SEWS IN AND OUT OF PENELOPE. 6
weeks: he learns Greek. It's
1856, just 100 years before

*

Penfield visions the brain
as Olduvai, digging
electrodes in to where
"now I hear people laughing, my friends, my
childhood friends"— "I see a man
with a pencil, this is
my first job." —"If these unimportant minutes of time
were preserved in the ganglionic recordings
of patients, why should it be thought that any
experience in the stream of consciousness fades
from the ganglionic record."

5.

Dear Tony:
Sky here's the color of cerebrum, but the outskirts
trees are carnelian, really, meat
reds, and some of those autumn corals have even invaded
the campus. There are beautiful gorges and
gorgeous beautifuls everywhere, though illness has kept me
from plunging into either. Dogs,
it's an old custom, are Cornell's sacred
cows, and wander the rows at poetry readings
like scansion. My classes

Dear Wayne:
sophomore level, untalented
but eager. And I'm left plenty of time. I write less,
what with the mono and all, but
consistently, and am fiddling around with more
goddam archaeologists. All
too sanctimonious pieces! As if . . . sort of
conjuring Syl; or having sun, like a word
in a bottle's neck, touch
off her voice in my skull; or just digging
open a letter from you

Dear Ginnie:
like excavation. And then I made notes, maybe
Burnt House On Etna Road —a new epic. Hey,
did you hear Maura won the Yale Prize?! Give
my regards to Tony, he's the only blossom
on the whole drab, lethal
poetry cactus in Utah!, and tell him to

Dear Alan:
write me. So many moments —something
I'm researching makes Penelope's
handiwork seem appropriate here— unweave
overnight, if we aren't fixative. Syl
sent the negatives:

Richard gagging, Michael cretinous under his beachcomber hat,
   you
staring as if you'd just eaten
an opium steak. I've been thinking of photos

   Dear Syl:
with your hair cascading thick,
black, and strong, like transoceanic
cables, and my left hand
cupping your tit. It's up on the kitchen wall.
And yesterday . . . well, there's this
suspension bridge, a flock of freshmen
girls were waddling their tooshies across, with occasional
terriers for punctuation, and then I thought —not
of the Duke-picture, but of *me*
thinking of the Duke-picture. It's . . . now
work hard to see this: the creek
below thrashed thick
buttermilk against rock outcrops, and
when I stopped to listen, sun cast
my head's shadow first on the bridge's chainlink side then, in
that frame, it was
caught a second time,
smaller, more sharp-edged, below on the gorgewall —and
there it was, one wide-eyed man's
gray image of himself seen taking shape, like a
remembering, in his own skull —and the whole
scene backdropped by tier on tier of geology! Surely
there's richness in that . . . If I get it
written, I'll send it to you. And you send me
your love, for my
                    Love,

                albert

6.

It's only dirt. And it's only dirt,
and the guide-boy waits at the bottom of it,
idly scraping his foot calloused
thick as shoeleather
in it, and watches him
take the hill. It's mid-day.
The olive leaves facet, and
throw, light
like a treasury. His linen suit
droops with the heat, but he writes Sophia his
resolve is beyond seasons. Goatstink,
cheap amphoras of lunchwine, the sudsing
edge of the island . . . This
is it. It's 1878, and Schliemann
❋

scrapes dirt from his first validating wedge of ancient
                                                    Ithaka.

7.

A man wakes. The weather's
a brain on the landscape.

It's central New York. In
and out, now
clear, now clouded, two
thrushes stitch gray sky.

Albert Goldbarth is a young poet who, after studying and teaching in Chicago, Iowa, and Utah, currently makes his home in Ithaca, New York. He is the author of eight volumes of poetry including *Comings Back* and *Jan. 31*, which was nominated for the 1975 National Book Award in poetry. New work is in progress.